BALANCE OF POWER

International Politics as the Ultimate Global Game

BY CHRIS CRAWFORD

BALANCE OF POWER

International Politics as the Ultimate Global Game

BY CHRIS CRAWFORD

Illustrations by David Shannon

MICROSOFT PRESS

PUBLISHED BY

Microsoft Press
A Division of Microsoft Corporation
16011 N.E. 36th, Box 97017
Redmond, Washington 98073-9717

Library of Congress Cataloging in Publication Data
Crawford, Chris, 1950-
Balance of power.
Bibliography: p.
1. Balance of power (Game)   2. International relations—Data
processing.   3. Macintosh (Computer)—Programming.
4. IBM Personal Computers—Programming.   I. Title.
GV1469.25.B34C73   1986   794.8'2   86-18195
ISBN 0-914845-97-7

Printed and bound in the United States of America.

1 2 3 4 5 6 7 8 9 FGFG 8 9 0 9 8 7 6

Distributed to the book trade in the
United States by Harper & Row.

Distributed to the book trade in
Canada by General Publishing Company, Ltd.

Distributed to the book trade outside the
United States and Canada by Penguin Books Ltd.

Penguin Books Ltd., Harmondsworth, Middlesex, England
Penguin Books Australia Ltd., Ringwood, Victoria, Australia
Penguin Books N.Z. Ltd., 182-190 Wairau Road, Auckland 10,
New Zealand

British Cataloging in Publication Data available

*D*EDICATION

To Kathy, my wife...

...and my cast of supporting critters: Betsy, Tom, Sally, Sherry, Sherlock, Sheeba, Ginger, Lucy, Bunny, Sammy, Sasha, Andy, Kiwi, Velvet, and Flannel.

TABLE OF CONTENTS

INTRODUCTION

I never dreamed while I was working on *Balance of Power* that I would someday be writing a book about it. The problems of writing a book about this game remind me of the problems of the military historian attempting to describe a battle. Battlefields are notoriously confusing places, for the people present are much too busy saving their skins and being terrified to clearly take note of events. The historian must distill a kaleidoscope of bullets, screaming, and blood into neat diagrams with arrows and boxes. I feel the same way about this book: It will undoubtedly make the game seem much more rationally prepared than was the case. Nevertheless, I accept the necessity of imposing order on a potpourri of random events that went to make up the finished game.

I wrote this book with three audiences in mind. The first audience is those persons who have purchased *Balance of Power*, played it, and thereby developed a curiosity about geopolitics. To this group I offer more information on geopolitics than I could put into the game's manual. I hope that the additional information in this book will increase their enjoyment of the game, and maybe even their scores. The second audience is composed of people moving in the opposite intellectual direction, from geopolitics to games. They know a great deal about the real world but are curious about the expression of real-world concepts in the alien medium of the computer. I tried to present the logic of this process in a fashion that would be understandable to a non-programmer. The third audience is those people who are curious about the game design process itself and want to follow the effort in detail. For these people I inserted occasional digressive paragraphs on the finer points of game design. I believe that the triply schizophrenic nature of the book does not interfere with its clarity; the transitions between personalities went so smoothly as to convince me that I am a truly polished madman.

Those readers who have not played *Balance of Power* can refer to the short description of the game provided in Chapter 1. I also provide an Appendix in which I play a sample game, complete with numerous screen dumps, comments on my thinking as I went through the game, and an endgame analysis of my mistakes.

I organized the main chapters around the central themes of the game: insurgencies, coups d'etat, Finlandization, and crises. Each of these chapters is broken into three parts. The first part provides the historical background on the topic. The second part describes the algorithms used in the game. The third part is a random collection of colorful tidbits and historical anecdotes generally related to the topic.

I chose to present the algorithms in an unconventional manner. The simplest and most direct solution would have been to reprint sections of the program listing. This would have had the added benefit of creating an aura of great authenticity to the descriptions. However, it suffers from two drawbacks. First, readers unfamiliar with the Pascal progamming language would have been unable to decipher the listings. Second, all readers would have been forced to struggle through the many trivial complexities of a real computer program. I wanted to discuss the ideas behind the game, not the dirty details of programming.

I therefore decided to present my equations in a sanitized format that should be intelligible to anybody with an understanding of high school algebra. I do not use short variable names like "x" or "y"; instead, I write out full names for every variable. For example, if we wanted to calculate a person's average income over the last two years, the traditional computer listing might read like this:

AveIncm := (Incm[t−1] + Incm[t]) div 2;

My own presentation of such an equation would read like this:

$$\textbf{Average Income} = \frac{\textbf{Last Year's Income} + \textbf{This Year's Income}}{\textbf{2}}$$

While this approach will fail to satisfy those few dedicated persons who want to delve into the innards of the program, I think it will satisfy the needs of the greater number of people who wish to understand the concepts behind the game.

Finally, I apologize to all those readers more knowledgeable about geopolitical matters than myself, who may wince at the necessary simplifications. I am first and foremost a game designer, not a political scientist. Simplification to achieve clarity is the essence of my work; clarity can be extracted from a muddy reality only by denying some of reality's richness.

BALANCE OF POWER
AND THE REAL WORLD

Balance of Power is a game about geopolitics in the nuclear age. You, the player, choose the role of President of the United States or General Secretary of the Soviet Union; the computer plays as the other leader. Your goal is to enhance your country's prestige. Prestige in *Balance of Power* is the extent to which your country is liked and respected by the other countries of the world, weighted by their respective military strengths. You want to have many powerful friends, but few and weak enemies.

3

The geopolitical stage is full of activity: All over the world, internal rumblings threaten the stability of almost every nation. Insurgencies develop to challenge governments with military action. Coups d'etat strike down the leadership of governments and install new leaders. Diplomatic intimidation induces weak nations to *Finlandize* to the superpowers, in the hope that an accommodating stance toward the powerful nation will prevent an attack.

These processes are the vehicles that you use to enhance your country's prestige. If an unfriendly government fights a desperate battle against guerrillas, you can provide weapons to the insurgents. If you are adventurous, you can even send your own troops into the country to intervene for the rebels ("freedom fighters"?). If the rebels succeed in overthrowing the government, their new regime will reward your assistance with friendly relations. Another unfriendly nation might be vulnerable to domestic destabilization; a judicious push by the CIA could topple the government and install a friendlier leader. Or perhaps a little diplomatic muscle-flexing could intimidate a small nation into a sensible Finlandization toward your country.

Of course, your computer opponent can take any of the same actions against your friends. To defend your friends, you have a number of options. You can help a friendly government with weapons shipments or even troop deployments (especially useful against insurgents). You can soothe domestic discontent with economic assistance which will bolster the regime against the possibility of a coup d'etat. Or you can sign a defense treaty with the nation, promising to aid it against any threat. This will enhance its confidence against attempts at intimidation by your opponent. Of course, you must honor your treaty commitments if they are to have any meaning.

You are free to engage in any of these policy actions anywhere in the world, as is your opponent. However, every move you make is subject to the acquiescence of your opponent. Should you perpetrate an action that your opponent finds objectionable, he might demand that you revoke your policy. This triggers the most dramatic moment of the game: the crisis. You can respond to his demand in one of two ways. You can accept his demand, back down, and countermand your action. Or you can stand firm and reject his demand, escalating the crisis to the next level. The ball goes to your opponent's court, where he must decide whether to back down himself, or emphasize his determination in the matter by escalating the crisis to an even higher level. This process of escalation or retreat continues until either one side backs down, or the crisis escalates to what is called *DefCon 1*. If one side does back down, it loses considerable prestige in the eyes of the world, for nations lose respect for a superpower that talks big but backs down in a crunch. If neither side backs down and DefCon 1 is reached, then the missiles are launched and the world is destroyed in a nuclear conflagration. Both sides lose.

Balance of Power is thus a game of judgment. In your role as a superpower leader, you must carefully gauge your opponent's likely response to every action you take. You must study the world situation carefully in order to be able to recognize those matters over which your opponent will not retreat. You must be able to differentiate these vital issues from opportunistic acts or bluffs on the part of your opponent.

To help the player in this effort, *Balance of Power* provides a mass of data on the nations of the world. A system of "smart maps" makes it easy to call up graphical representations of the state of insurgency, domestic discontent, diplomatic affinity, and many more variables for each nation of the world. (If you want to know how many television sets there are in Zambia, the figure is provided.)

The end result is a game that is complex and difficult. The richness of detail creates a compelling impression of verisimilitude. But there is a vast difference between the impression of verisimilitude and its reality. Just how accurate is this game in modeling the dynamics of geopolitical processes?

The complete answer to that question will take another five chapters. In this chapter, I wish to present some introductory thoughts on the problem of realism in *Balance of Power*. With this as an orientation, the reader will be better prepared to digest the material in the following chapters.

GAMES VERSUS SIMULATIONS

The first source of confusion that trips up many people is the difference between a game and a simulation. Most people do not trace any clear distinction between the two. Since the true meaning of a word is defined by the perceptions of the people who use the word, it is not possible for me to authoritatively define the ultimate, true, and final meaning of the word *game*. However, the word has taken so broad a meaning as to lose its utility, so I feel some justification in attempting to more precisely fix my use of the word. Moreover, when the ambiguity of a word contributes to confusion, any attempt at clarification is justified.

Games and simulations are similar in that they attempt to represent reality, but they differ in the intentions of their designers. A simulation is a serious attempt to represent the operation of some system with a verisimilitude that the most knowledgeable experts on the system would find acceptable. A simulation is often created with the intention of predicting the behavior of the system under situations not otherwise obtainable. For example, aircraft designers use computer simulations in the early stages of their work to test their ideas. It is much cheaper to simulate the behavior of an aircraft in a computer than to build the aircraft, watch it crash, and go back to the drawing board. Similarly, designers of nuclear weapons rely heavily on simulations to refine their designs. It's difficult to find spare cities laying around on which to test one's newest 20 megaton H-bomb. So they try it out on the computer.

Another common use of the simulation is for training purposes. The military has used simulations since their creation in the 1830s by a Prussian staff officer. On a large table with markers representing military units, officers consulting a detailed manual of rules maneuvered their armies in imaginary campaigns. The training value of such simulations was scoffed at by other armies until 1866 and 1870, when the Prussian army smashed first the Austro-Hungarian army and then the French army in two stunning campaigns. The rest of the world very quickly adopted the use of military simulations. An unfortunate problem in translation, though, has been the source of some confusion. The German term for these simulations is *Kriegspiel*, which can be translated literally as "war-play," and was translated into English as "wargame." However, the German word did not carry with it the connotation of frivolity that the English word carries. Certainly the German approach to the simulation, with its huge array of formidable rules and its unyielding emphasis on their precise application, and the grim mien with which the German staff officers approached their

Kriegspiel, would contradict any thought that this was playful activity.

Simulations are also used in business training. The aspiring executive can make her mistakes more cheaply in the confines of a simulation. She can try different marketing strategies, variations in the mount of money invested in research and development or manufacturing, and see how well her simulated company fares against its competition. The simulation allows one to see the complex interrelationships in any functioning business more clearly. It also provides a common basis for thinking within the organization. If all the executives in a company have experienced the same simulation, they have a better basis for communicating their thought processes to each other.

In all these cases, a dominant factor in the utility of the simulation is its *verisimilitude in detail.* The simulation must accurately predict the lift of the new aircraft's wing—if it is wrong, the airplane might crash. If the nuclear weapons simulation miscalculates the neutron budget of the hydrogen bomb, it might not detonate in combat; this would create an acute embarrassment to its designers. If the business simulation leads its students to misjudge their advertising budgets, their companies could go out of business. In all cases, the simulations are required to correctly predict a great many details. In most cases, these details are expected to be numeric quantities.

A game is dramatically different in its intentions. A game is to a simulation as a painting is to a blueprint. A painting of a house gives you an emotional impression of the house; a blueprint of the house tells the carpenter exactly where to put the windowsill. A game is no mere approximation of a simulation or a lower-quality version of a simulation. Instead, a game focuses on presenting broader, less quantifiable concepts. One would not use a painting as the basis for building a house, nor would one use a blueprint to convey his feelings about the house in which he spent his childhood. The difference is a matter of "soft concepts" versus "hard concepts"—those things that cannot be measured as opposed to those things that can. A simulation and a game attempt to communicate entirely different messages. The simulation communicates technical information, while a game communicates something closer to an artistic message.

COMPLICATIONS

In actual practice, the "information versus art" distinction between simulations and games is muddied by a variety of additional considerations. Consider, for example, a low-cost entertainment flight simulator commonly available for microcomputers. Surely the fundamental factors calculated by the program are no different than those modeled by the multi-million dollar professional flight simulators. Even a consumer flight simulator must calculate lift, altitude, airspeed, and the like. How, then, is it different from a professional flight simulator?

The answer lies in my earlier phrase "verisimilitude of detail." If your simulated aircraft is moving at an altitude of 8,000 feet, with a bank of 30 degrees and an airspeed of 180 knots, the microcomputer flight simulator is under no obligation to calculate the resultant lift with any great accuracy. If it makes some approximations here and there, if it cuts a few corners, nobody will be upset with it. By contrast, the professional simulator had better compute the lift accurately—that is its only reason to exist! If a pilot training on a professional flight simulator learns an incorrect response to a problem because of a flaw in the simulator, he could repeat the mistake in a real aircraft and jeopardize people's lives.

This is one reason why professional flight simulators require large and powerful computers with lots of RAM, while entertainment flight simulators can operate on microcomputers with far less power. It takes a lot of computer horsepower to compute all the little details correctly. A simulation running on a mere microcomputer must cut a few corners.

The home flight simulator faces a set of requirements that is different but not lesser than that of the professional product. The home flight simulator must create the illusion of accuracy, not its substance. A great deal of effort must be expended to create that illusion, to orchestrate the small visual or mental cues that will convince the user to suspend his disbelief. The user must, at some emotional level, believe that he is not sitting at the keyboard of his computer, but flying an airplane.

This requirement does imply that a certain level of accuracy be achieved. When the player puts the plane into a dive, it had better accelerate. But the exact rate of acceleration is utterly unimportant to the home user. More important would be the sound of the wind rushing by the cockpit faster and faster and the scream of the engine as the plane picks up speed. The simulation designer regards such factors as secondary and concentrates attention on the rate of acceleration. But the game designer sweats blood over the creation of his illusion.

Another difference between the game and the simulation arises from the player's expectation of a clear conflict. In the real world, conflict is tamed by a variety of social inhibitions. Conflict exists and is unavoidable in a wide range of human activities, but we have developed a complex array of mores and psychological repressions that soften the conflict and divert it to productive ends. The businessman snarls, "Let's get out there and sell so many units that the competition won't know what hit 'em!" While these mores make possible our civilization, they grate against a physiology that is adapted to resolving conflicts with claw and tooth, not a handshake and a smile. There thus exists a craving for entertainment that provides simple, direct conflict with simple, violent resolution. Any game that hopes to achieve commercial success must accentuate the conflict and remove the inhibitions that frustrate our bloodlust. This does not mean that all games must be blood-soaked shoot-'em-ups. They must, however, clarify and emphasize the conflict inherent in the situation and provide the emotionally satisfying resolution that our real-world conflicts so often lack.

A third differentiating factor is the accessibility of the game. A simulation need not balk at requiring its users to study long documents or undergo lengthy preparations. A game, on the other hand, must be immediately accessible to its user. Consumers will not tolerate a game that requires them to read long, boring manuals before they can derive any benefit from it. In this respect, *Balance of Power* is one of the most demanding games in the marketplace, for its hefty manual is a necessary component of the game.

IMPLICATIONS FOR A GAME MODELING GEOPOLITICS

The considerations discussed so far make it possible to understand the basis for answering the question, "How realistic is *Balance of Power?*" The fact that it is a game does not mean that it must be fundamentally inaccurate; it is, after all, a representation of reality. But it will necessarily distort reality in a variety of ways. For example, the game accentuates the conflict in the geopolitical scene and presents a simplified view of the complex processes of the real world. These are distortions of reality but they do not make the game untruthful. A good portrait painter accentuates those facial features that reveal character and simplifies away those features that compromise his representation; in the process, the painter distorts reality to reveal truth, not deny it.

Consider, for example, a very simple question: How many of the world's countries should be represented in the game? At first blush, most people would declare that *all* the world's countries should be included in the game. That certainly seems to be the safest and most accurate answer. But this is a game about geopolitical interactions; the question is, would the inclusion of all countries enhance or obscure the clarity of presentation of geopolitical interactions? A great many of the 150 countries of the world spend long decades in peaceful obscurity before some chance event propels them onto the world stage. How many Americans had heard of Grenada before the American invasion? How many Americans have heard of such countries as Cabinda, Andorra, San Marino, Oman, Burundi, Guinea-Bissau, or Gabon? How many know the difference between Mauritania and Mauritius? Would learning about all these tiny countries add to one's understanding of grand geopolitical forces, or would it distract one's attention from such forces?

The geopolitical system consists of two superpowers, a dozen major powers, a few dozen minor powers, and a host of non-powers. The role played by the non-powers in the geopolitical arena is little more than that of a pawn. Any game purporting to illuminate the nature of geopolitical processes must focus primarily on the superpowers. Such a game must obviously have *some* pawns for the superpowers to squabble over, but their role will always be minor.

In designing *Balance of Power*, I decided that the inclusion of too many non-powers would be detrimental to a game, even though it would be a positive factor in a simulation, so I settled on a final count of only 62 countries. Verisimilitude of detail is desirable in a simulation, so more countries add to the value of a simulation. But the inclusion of many non-powers in a game would only create a distraction. An excessive number of tiny countries in *Balance of Power* would be like verbiage in a sentence, clutter on a desk, or busyness in an image.

RELATIVE REALISM

The final general point I must make about the realism of the game is that the concept of realism is always measured relative to the perceptions of the viewer. A professor of political science will necessarily view the game in an entirely different light than a twelve-year-old. The level of accuracy of the game must be gauged against the intellectual background of its likely audience. This is one of the reasons that I chose the Macintosh as the initial target machine—my hunch was that the Macintosh audience would be an intellectually mature group. A complex game such as *Balance of Power* demands a great deal of intellectual effort from its players.

The game designer must pick a target level of realism appropriate to his audience. By doing so, he gains the scorn of those more educated than his target and loses the comprehension of those less educated than his target. The distribution of education in a large population being what it is, most game designers tend to target toward a sixth-grade education. It takes a strong-willed (in the words of one editor, "fanatic and obstinate") game designer to shoot for a college level of education in his game.

I must admit that I aimed a little too high with *Balance of Power.* I assumed a good deal more understanding of geopolitical issues of the average American computer owner than appears to be the case. Many players seem to regard the game as unwinnable. This has been a source of dismay and embarrassment to me.

"REALISM AS PROCESS" VERSUS "REALISM AS DATA"

Another important consideration regarding the nature of realism concerns the realism of the process as opposed to the realism of the data. Most people think of realism in terms of data. They ask if the Gross National Product is correctly reported, or if the number of troops in this country is accurate. But data is not the most important element in realism—process is. Thoreau made the point in *Walden*:

> *If we read of one man robbed, or murdered, or killed by accident, or one house burned, or one vessel wrecked, or one steamboat blown up, or one cow run over on the Western railroad, or one mad dog killed, or one lot of grasshoppers in the winter—we need never read of another. One is enough. If you are acquainted with the principle, what do you care for a myriad of instances and applications?*

What is important is the principle, not the instance, and principles are processes. The actual amount of the GNP of Ghana is less important, for the purposes of a game on geopolitics, than the manner in which that GNP changes with time. The fact that Nicaragua has poor diplomatic relations with Washington is less important than the reasons *why* Nicaragua has poor diplomatic relations with Washington. You can't interact with a fact. It's like a dead fish—it just lays there. But you can interact with a process. You can shape it, change the parameters that affect its behavior. Ultimately, you can learn about it. Facts are best relegated to books and other static media, and computers are best applied to problems involving processes, for computers are not "*data* processors" but "data *processors.*"

Processes are the *real* stuff of the world. If we have the wisdom to survive the next 100 years, our descendents will look back on our squabbles with Nicaragua as so much irrelevant nonsense. But the same principles, the same processes that govern our relationship with Nicaragua, will still be in force. More than two thousand years ago, the Greek historian Thucydides, writing about the Peloponnesian War, said, "What made war inevitable was the growth of Athenian power and the fear which this caused in Sparta." Replace "Athenian" with "American" and "Sparta" with "Russia" and you may have our epitaph. The facts of Athens and Sparta are dust, but the principles have not changed.

This concept—which I call *process intensity*—is the organizing principle of this book. The chapters focus on the four processes of geopolitical interaction that I chose to emphasize in the game: insurgency, coups d'etat, Finlandization, and crises. I give the facts themselves short shrift. Facts are transitory, while processes are the enduring truths.

A number of people have asked if I plan to prepare an update to the game, incorporating the latest changes in the international scene. They seem to believe that events like the fall of Marcos and the American attacks on Libya somehow change the circumstances of the game. These events change only the cosmetics of the game, not its substance. *Balance of Power* is a game about geopolitical interaction, the principles of which have not changed fundamentally since the introduction of the nuclear-tipped ICBM. It would take but a few hours' work to rearrange the game to include the events of the last year. For that matter, it would not take much more time to make the game cover the period of the 1960s. In the last twenty-five years the details have changed but the principles have not, and *Balance of Power* is a game about principles, not details. I have no plans for any updates, for there is nothing in the game to update.

*R*EALISM AND LEARNING

If the realism of the game is measured relative to the level of expertise of the perceiver, then it follows that the learning process of the game must itself make the game seem less realistic. That is, the beginning player will accord the game a great deal of respect, but as he plays the game and learns the principles behind it, his growing understanding of geopolitical processes will make it easier for him to see the flaws in the design. This is a natural and predictable phenomenon, and is in fact the best measure of success of the game. A game that fails to change its player is a failure. A game should lift the player up to higher levels of understanding; in the process, the player who once stood at its feet later stands on its shoulders.

THE WONDERFUL WORLD OF INSURGENCY

An insurgency is an armed attempt by native elements acting outside the government to overthrow the government or repudiate its control over a region. It is characterized by a protracted campaign between the armed forces of the state and those of the insurgency. An insurgency is differentiated from a coup d'etat by the facts that a coup is a very sudden event and one that often involves persons working from within the machinery of the government.

Insurgency is as old as the institutions of government; presumably the act of asserting governmental authority over a group creates the possibility that they will violently resist that authority. But the postwar era has seen a new dimension added to insurgency. It is now used by the superpowers as a vehicle for furthering their own geopolitical interests. The revulsion that nations of the world have developed for blatant imperialism has forced the superpowers to take their imperialism underground and cloak it in more "respectable" garb. The native insurgency offers a superpower an ideal opportunity to further its own interests while playing the role of benefactor rather than invader. Insurgency is thus the first vehicle of competition in *Balance of Power.*

PRIMARY INGREDIENTS

Three primary ingredients are necessary to cook up an insurgency. First, you must have a government or other legitimate authority against whom the insurgency is directed. After all, you can't have a rebellion against no one! Second, you must have the insurgents themselves: the people who rebel against the government. Third, the insurgents must be willing to use armed force against the government. The element of armed force is not necessary to ensure success (witness Mohandas Gandhi), but without it you have civil disobedience or a coup d'etat, not an insurgency.

THE GOVERNMENT

The first ingredient in this ugly stew is the government. The government seems to hold all the cards. It has a great deal of military power at its disposal, in the form of the regular armed forces. Contrary to common

American beliefs, the armed forces of most Third World nations exist not to defend against external enemies, but to keep the local population under control.

For most of history, these nations did not need much in the way of armed forces to maintain order. A few thousand troops armed with rifles were sufficient to contain almost any situation. When you remember that the average peasant had little weaponry, the poor state of Third World armies makes a great deal of sense. But since World War II, we have seen a dramatic leap in the size of Third World armies and the weapons available to them. Part of this is due to increases in population, but the superpowers have played a major role in militarizing the Third World nations. By making them the arena for superpower competition, they have forced these nations to arm themselves heavily. Guerrillas armed with surface-to-air missiles and semi-automatic assault rifles can only be combated with pretty hefty military forces. Unfortunately, when all this firepower is unleashed among large numbers of ignorant peasants, it is the peasants who take most of the casualties.

The second advantage of the government is legitimacy. Any government, no matter how corrupt or oppressive, has a tremendous moral advantage over those who would overthrow it. A government represents law and order, civilization, and stability. Those citizens who don't want to be bothered will support the government, if only by their inactivity.

The third advantage of the government is its control of the nation's infrastructure—the web of basic services such as transportation, communication, and medical services that are essential for carrying on a protracted conflict. Against this well-established infrastructure the insurgents are hard pressed to communicate with each other, move troops and weapons, provide medical care for their wounded, and spread their propaganda to the masses.

THE INSURGENTS

Against the government are pitted the insurgents. The first question that occurs to most people about insurgents is, "Why would anybody take on such a formidable power? What motivates people to engage in such seemingly hopeless efforts?"

There are many reasons for insurgency. In modern times we most often hear of the "social revolution"—a revolution that seeks to supplant an oppressive social order with a supposedly more enlightened one. A large number of left-wing insurgencies operate under this banner.

But there are other motivations for insurgency. A common one is separatism, the desire of one social group to break loose from its political ties with the larger nation. If the group is large enough, and its cultural or geographical differences with the parent state great enough, then we call such separatist sentiments "nationalist."

For example, the Irish insurgency against Britain was, throughout most of its course, primarily nationalistic in sense. The early economic depredations that the English had visited upon the Irish had slowly abated, until by the time of the final break, there were plausible arguments that a break with England would be economically disadvantageous to the Irish. Yet nationalism was not to be denied. The Irish break with England did make cultural and geographic sense, since the Irish differed from the English in religion, language, history, culture, and geography. This was a clean, nationalistic break.

22

On the other hand we have Catalonia, a portion of Spain. Catalonians consider themselves distinct from the rest of Spain, but in language and culture the distinction is not so great as that between the Irish and the English. More important, Catalonia could not function as a separate economy; its economy is too closely woven into the fabric of the entire Spanish economy. Thus, efforts directed toward Catalonian autonomy are more separatist than nationalist.

Religious factors, too, can play a role in insurgency. Westerners may think of religious insurgency in terms of recent expressions of Islamic extremism, but religious factors played a large role in insurgencies during the Reformation and were the primary expression of insurgency during Roman times. It is not that religion exerted life-and-death influence over people's hearts and minds in these societies; it's just that churches were the primary locus of social activity in these societies. Were a major insurgency to form in the United States, it would probably be based in shopping malls.

A final motivation for insurgency is anti-colonialist sentiment. This is often closely associated with a developing sense of nationalism, but is more economic in flavor. The revolt of the American colonies against England was more anti-colonialist than nationalist. Many of the Founding Fathers considered themselves loyal Englishmen, but they could not acquiesce to the continuing economic penalties that the mother country exacted from them.

These motivations are often mixed in any real insurgency. For example, the Vietnamese insurgency of 1945-75 started out primarily as a nationalistic uprising, an assertion of Vietnamese national identity. The Japanese had done a great deal of propagandizing during World War II to present their war as a crusade of Asian against

Westerner, and the propaganda left a mark in Vietnam. There was also a goodly dose of anticolonialism mixed in, for the French had not been the most benign of imperial powers. Only later, when Ho Chi Minh began to seek foreign support, did he seriously add a social agenda to his insurgency. His shift toward communism was primarily to curry favor with the Chinese and Soviets. There is nothing unique about this—insurgency leaders have been notoriously fluid in their ideological foundations. After all, when you're running an insurgency, you find it difficult to recruit people to risk near-certain death for a highly dubious proposition. So, it's nice to be able to spice up your insurgency with an enticing menu of causes to get the maximum number of recruits.

ARMED FORCE

Recruitment is at once the greatest weakness and the greatest strength of any insurgency. The government can draft all the soldiers it needs, albeit of dubious quality and motivation. The insurgency is not so lucky. You can kidnap a bunch of people, and it is often attempted, but all too frequently the soldiers you shanghai run away at the worst possible moment, taking precious guns and ammunition with them. Most insurgencies must therefore run on volunteer power. That's tough—not many people are hot to die for a cause. On the other hand, insurgency soldiers are usually better motivated than the government troops they fight. The typical government conscript would much rather loaf around in the barracks than rummage around in the bush getting shot at. The typical insurgency fighter is there to fight.

The insurgency has one other advantage, and it is a huge one: It has the initiative. The insurgents decide how, when, and where they will strike; the government can do very little until they act. The insurgents can remain hidden, looking for a weak spot, and then hit when they have local superiority. In this manner, a small force of insurgents can inflict repeated defeats on a much larger government force. This is the one factor that makes insurgency so effective in so many situations.

DEVELOPMENT OF AN INSURGENCY

Let's trace the history of a hypothetical generic insurgency. The story always starts with a government that is not totally popular with the people—this includes just about every government in human history. Some malcontents are angry enough to do something about it. Initially, opposition to the government is scattered; the various malcontents are all isolated from one another and unable to communicate.

TERRORISM

The first step comes when some hothead carries out an act of violence against the government. It is necessarily rather puny; after all, we can't expect every hothead to have much military power at his disposal (thank heaven!). This act, however, serves to galvanize opposition. Once people realize that there are others willing to fight back, they gravitate toward each other and the insurgency begins to take shape. During this early stage, the insurgents still lack any real military power. They operate as part-time rebels, living during the day as regular citizens, but plotting their revolution in secrecy and making occasional strikes. This stage of an evolving insurgency is characterized in *Balance of Power* as terrorism.

GUERRILLA WAR

After a while, the terrorists establish a macabre sort of credibility by blowing up enough innocents. People start to fear and resent them, but they take them seriously as a real challenge to the government. As their credibility grows, they attract more recruits and possibly some weapons from a foreign source, most likely a superpower on the make. If all goes well, they graduate to the next level of insurgency: guerrilla warfare. Three factors differentiate the guerrilla from the terrorist. First, the guerrilla is normally a full-time operator while the terrorist is more likely a part-timer. Second, guerrillas tend to live together in camps, while terrorists more often split up in small groups. Finally, guerrillas normally operate in a rural environment, leaving the cities and towns to the government, while the terrorist is more of an urban animal.

CIVIL WAR

If the guerrilla war goes well, it will eventually graduate to the highest level of insurgency, the civil war. This requires the guerrillas to gain so much military power that they can stand up to the government forces in direct combat. Three factors differentiate a civil war from a guerrilla war. The first is the military power of the insurgents. Guerrillas can operate successfully with only a small fraction of the military power available to the government, but in a civil war, the force ratio is much closer to 1:1. The second indicator of a civil war is the fact that the insurgents are able to control territory. Guerrillas may be able to operate freely in certain regions of a country, but they cannot claim to openly control land, for the government can occupy and hold any location it desires. In a civil war, this is no longer true; the rebels are able to assert control over a portion of the national territory and the government does not have the strength to oust them. This gives rise to the third distinguishing trait of a civil war: the claim to legitimacy. The rebels form a "provisional revolutionary government" and advance the claim that their government is indeed the true and proper government of the nation.

INTERNATIONAL RECOGNITION

At this point a very tricky issue arises: international recognition. The old government claims that *it* is the true and proper government of the nation; the provisional revolutionary government claims that status for itself. The issue will probably be decided on the battlefield, but in the interim, whom will the other nations of the world believe? The matter is of great significance for several reasons. First, recognition by foreign nations confers great prestige upon a provisional revolutionary government and goes a long way toward swaying undecided citizens. A civil war is a battle for the hearts and minds of the nation, and prestige is as much a weapon as artillery. If a series of nations abandon the old government and recognize the rebels as the legitimate government, this creates a momentum of prestige that operates against the old government.

A second major consequence of recognition is that it legitimatizes a greater level of military assistance to the rebels. Providing weapons or, worse, troops to an insurgency is generally recognized as a dirty business; a superpower must accept a certain amount of international opprobrium for such behavior, since it is undeniably meddling in the internal affairs of a nation against the wishes of the legitimate government. However, the situation changes dramatically once the superpower has recognized the provisional revolutionary government. It can now claim that it is only assisting the legitimate government of the country, at the express request of that government.

This may sound like so much diplomatic double-talk, but there is a great deal of substance to it. You see, a nation cannot recognize *two* governments for one country; the act of recognizing the provisional revolutionary government necessitates withdrawal of recognition from the old government. This requires the foreign power to withdraw its ambassador to the old government and terminate diplomatic relations. This step is fraught with risk. If the old government wins the civil war, the nation that severed diplomatic relations will be caught in an embarrassing position. Moreover, for the duration of the civil war, it will have no means of furthering its interests with the old government. None of the normal diplomatic housekeeping that goes on between nations will be possible. For this reason, most nations are quite conservative about recognizing new governments; they will wait until victory has clearly gone to the rebels before recognizing the new government.

Sometimes a nation will withhold diplomatic recognition for reasons of policy. For example, the civil war in China led to an outright communist victory in 1949; the Nationalist forces fled to the island of Taiwan. At this point, most nations of the world recognized the communist government as the legitimate government of China. However, the United States had made strong commitments to the Nationalists, and refused to recognize the communist government. For nearly thirty years, we operated under the apparently ridiculous position that a group of bandits had seized control of a part of China (the mainland), but the *real* government continued to operate in Taipei. This policy arose not from stupidity but from our refusal to abandon a down-but-not-out ally. What good are our commitments to our other allies if they know that the USA abandons its commitments when the going gets rough? After a decent interval of several decades, we could back off from the Nationalist government without overmuch damage to our credibility.

THE ROLE OF THE SUPERPOWERS

Insurgency would be a much more difficult game if it were not for the meddling of the superpowers. Since World War II, there have been very few insurgencies that did not in some way benefit from the aid of a major power. Sometimes this aid is limited and indirect. The Soviet Union sometimes funnels small quantities of weapons to minor terrorist groups through a variety of middlemen. More often, the aid is provided without such attempts at concealment, such as the American aid to the contras of Nicaragua.

PROVIDING WEAPONS

Support in the form of weapons shipments is vital to the progress of an insurgency, for the weapons directly available to insurgents are not adequate to the task at hand. The central tactical maneuver of all insurgents is to carefully concentrate their power on a vulnerable target, pour large quantities of firepower onto the target from a safe distance, and then melt away. The ideal weapon for such an attack is an assault rifle, a semi-automatic rifle that can fire lots of rounds quickly. The problem for most insurgents is that an assault rifle has absolutely no civilian use, and hence is banned in most of the world. Insurgents who must make do with civilian weapons such as pistols and hunting rifles simply cannot bring much firepower to bear, and are easily out-gunned by just a few soldiers armed with proper weapons.

The good news, then, is that insugencies cannot prosper without weapons shipments. The bad news is that such shipments are easily obtained. The United States alone has produced more than 6,000,000 M1 carbines, 3,500,000 M16s, and 1,500,000 M14s. That is 10 million weapons for a country with only 2 million soldiers. A great many of these weapons have made their way into the shadowy international arms market. When South Vietnam fell, for example, Hanoi captured nearly a million American M16s. When you have millions of loose weapons running around the world, it is not difficult for a few thousand to make their way to any given insurgency.

A typical assault rifle with a small stock of ammunition costs about $300. Thus, a superpower can set up an insurgency with quite an arsenal for less than a million dollars. In the inflated world of arms procurements, that's loose change. And it buys a lot of power. In terms of projecting power around the world, arming insurgents is far and away the most cost-effective way for a superpower to throw its weight around. That's why it's done so often.

PROVIDING SOLDIERS

Of course, there is another way for a superpower to involve itself in an insurgency, and that is to directly intervene in the fighting with its own forces. This is far more effective than weapons shipments. As it happens, most armies of the world are hopelessly ineffective, at least when compared to the armies of the superpowers. Their soldiers just can't seem to get into the spirit of things. Thus, the injection of well-trained superpower troops can have a dramatic impact on the course of the fighting. However, intervention is politically and diplomatically a sensitive action, and so most interventions are sharply limited in both size and the freedom of action accorded the combatants; this has tended to cancel out the advantages of the superpower's superior troops. The American interventions in Vietnam and Lebanon are generally regarded as failures. The Soviet intervention in Afghanistan has, so far, not been able to secure victory.

INSURGENCY IN BALANCE OF POWER

Balance of Power must calculate the behavior of the insurgency in each country of the world. This means that it must first calculate the strength of the insurgency and the strength of the government forces. It must then determine how these two forces fare in combat with each other. Then it must determine the significance of this outcome, such as whether the insurgency has graduated to the status of a civil war. Finally, the program must compute the consequences of an insurgency victory on the makeup of the government and its relationships with the superpowers.

There are a number of special terms that must be defined before I can present the equations used in *Balance of Power.* The first of these are:

Soldiers—simply the number of soldiers that the government has in its army;

Weapons—the amount of government money spent on weapons;

Military Aid—the amount of weapons received from superpowers by the government;

Government Power—the net military power that results from these soldiers and weapons;

Intervention Power—the military power provided by any intervening superpower troops.

The equation that determines the military power of the government is:

Total Weapons = Weapons + Military Aid

$$\textbf{Government Power} = \frac{\textbf{(2 * Soldiers * Total Weapons)}}{\textbf{(Soldiers + Total Weapons)}} + \textbf{Intervention Power}$$

This equation says two things: First, more soldiers means more power; second, more total weapons means more power. That's natural and obvious. What is special about this equation is the way that it creates a natural balance between weapons and soldiers. Suppose, for example, that we have a country like China that has lots of soldiers but not many weapons. Suppose that the values for China are 100 soldiers and a total of 2 weapons. This would yield a total power of 3. Now comes the good part. Suppose that the Chinese added one more soldier; how would that increase their power? Well, if you try the equation with 101 soldiers and 2 total weapons, you still get a total power of only 3. Now suppose that the Chinese added one more weapon instead of one more soldier; then their military power would jump up to 5. The moral of this equation is that you need a proper balance between soldiers and weapons. If you have too many of either, it doesn't hurt you, but you just don't get much benefit from the additional resource.

The military power of the insurgency (*Insurgency Power*) is computed in a similar manner, except that the number of insurgency fighters and the amount of insurgency weaponry must be computed in a different fashion. The number of fighters in the insurgency is based on three factors: the *population* of the country, the *maturity* of the political institutions in the country, and the degree of *success* of the insurgency. These last two require some explanation.

Why is it that so many Third World nations seem to be caught in a perpetual cycle of violence? Whichever side is in power must torture and kill its opponents, while the opponents carry on a violent resistance. We Westerners shake our heads in dismay at the senseless violence and, perhaps, indulge in the vanity that we are spared such bloodshed because we are in some way superior. Our advantage lies in the stability of our cultural and governmental institutions. Our civilization has not known outright anarchy for more than a thousand years. We have slowly built up a common understanding as to what is fair and proper in societal behavior. When Richard Nixon resigned the Presidency, people didn't grab their guns and head for the streets—we all shared a common respect for the institutions of our society and a confidence that our own interests would be protected by those institutions. That confidence has been developed over a thousand years of steadily growing lawfulness.

Such is not the case with many countries of the world. Many of the sub-Saharan nations have no tradition of strong legal institutions before 1960. While we were struggling with the Magna

Carta and developing concepts of representative government, they were still digging their way out of the Bronze Age. They may sit down at the parliamentary table to play by the rules, but they keep their hands close to their guns. And why shouldn't they? What basis do they have for trusting each other?

This vitally important element is encoded in *Balance of Power* as an array called *Maturity*. The values are encoded at the beginning of the game and remain constant throughout the game. Serious students of political history will be dismayed to learn that I simply fabricated these values. I had to—there were none available. After all, what respectable scholar would attempt anything so arrogant as to quantify the level of lawfulness of each nation of the world? So I relied on my vast knowledge of world affairs (ahem!) and performed a feat of prestidigitation. Some sample values used in the game are:

Country	Maturity Value
USA	240
Mexico	130
Panama	34
France	226
Italy	218
Egypt	74
Mali	24
Zaire	32
Japan	220
China	100
Saudi Arabia	40
Philippines	80

There is, of course, plenty of room for argument about these numbers. I gave them a great deal of thought but cannot produce justification for any single number.

The second factor in the recruitment rate for insurgency is the degree of success of the insurgency. This is a variation on the bandwagon effect. Nobody wants to have any part of a losing proposition, especially when losers get shot, but once the insurgents start to rack up some victories, the hopes of the discontented start to outweigh their fears, and recruitment picks up.

Put it all together, and we have a pair of formulae for the number of fighters available to an insurgency:

$$\text{Success} = \frac{\text{square root of (6400 * Last Year's Insurgency Power)}}{\text{Last Year's Government Power}}$$

$$\text{Fighters} = \frac{((256 - \text{Maturity}) * \text{Population} * \text{Success})}{20480}$$

Insurgency weaponry is computed in a different fashion. Insurgents don't have taxes or a military budget; they instead scrape together weapons from the international black market or whatever they can steal from the government. Their main source of weapons is always a Sugar Daddy superpower. In the rare absence of such a benefactor, thy make do. Since insurgents tend to fight in a manner less dependent on weaponry, my formula compensates for this:

Insurgency Weapons = 2 * Weapons Shipments from Superpowers

$$\text{IF Insurgency Weapons} < \frac{\text{Fighters}}{8} + 1 \text{ THEN Insurgency Weapons} = \frac{\text{Fighters}}{8} + 1$$

The first equation doubles the effective value of any weapons shipped to the insurgents. This is because insurgents tend to extract greater value from their weapons than government soldiers do. Since they have so little, they use it more carefully. The second formula says that if the insurgents are getting very few weapons compared to the number of fighters they have, then they scrounge up whatever they can, which isn't much.

We can now compute the value of insurgency power with this formula:

$$\text{Insurgency Power} = \frac{(2 * \text{Fighters} * \text{Insurgency Weapons})}{\text{Fighters} + \text{Insurgency Weapons}} + \text{Intervention Power}$$

This equation is analogous to the equation for government power and operates in the same fashion. In this case, intervention power applies only to those superpower troops who intervene in favor of the insurgency.

The next task is to let the insurgency and the government shoot each other up for a year's time and ask how much damage they inflict on each other in that time. Now, calculations of this nature can be quite involved. Many experts spend a great deal of time trying to develop such *combat results systems*. One American expert, Colonel Trevor Dupuy (U.S. Army, Ret.), has devoted many years to studying the problem. My approach is, by such standards, ridiculously oversimplified. But *Balance of Power* is not a game about combat, it is a game about geopolitics, and I felt a need to keep my combat results systems simple. I therefore settled on the following very simple system:

$$\text{Government Power} = \text{Government Power} - \frac{\text{Insurgency Power}}{4}$$

$$\text{Insurgency Power} = \text{Insurgency Power} - \frac{\text{Government Power}}{4}$$

These equations mean that the amount of damage that each side can inflict on the other is equal to one-quarter of its own strength. The more powerful the government is, the more insurgents get killed, and the more powerful the insurgency is, the more government troops get killed. If they are both powerful, then lots of people die.

This done, we are ready to see how well the insurgency is doing. The ratio of government strength to insurgency strength tells the story. If the ratio is greater than 512, then the government has everything under control and *Balance of Power* calls it peace. If the ratio is less than 512 but greater than 32, then we call it terrorism, and if the ratio is less than 32 but greater than 2, we call it guerrilla war. If the ratio is between 1 and 2, then we call it a civil war. And, should the ratio of government strength to insurgency strength ever fall below 1, then the rebels are stronger than the government and they win. When this happens, a whole host of changes take place. The insurgency trades places with the government; the old oppressors take to the hills and yesterday's freedom fighters enjoy the satisfying sound of the whip cracking in their own hands. If either superpower had intervened in favor of the insurgents in the civil war, then the insurgents gratefully compromise their political values to be more in tune with those of their beneficiary:

IF USA intervened for insurgency THEN Government Wing =

$$\frac{\textbf{(Government Wing + USA Government Wing)}}{\textbf{2}}$$

IF USSR intervened for insurgency THEN Government Wing =

$$\frac{\textbf{(Government Wing + USSR Government Wing)}}{\textbf{2}}$$

In this equation, the term *Government Wing* refers to the political leaning of the government, with an extremely left-wing government having a value of -128, an extremely right-wing government taking a value of $+128$, and a moderate government taking a value of 0. *USA Government Wing* is the political leaning of the government of the United States, which I set at about 20, while I set *USSR Government Wing* to -80.

The new government starts with a clean slate in its relations with the populace; its initial popularity decreases with the extremity of its political philosophy:

$$\textbf{Popularity = 10} + \frac{\textbf{(128 − Abs(Government Wing))}}{\textbf{2}}$$

Government popularity is important for determining the likelihood of a coup d'etat and will be discussed in the next chapter.

Next, we must calculate the state of diplomatic relations between the new revolutionary government and the superpowers. This will be based on the political leanings of the new government as compared with the political leanings of the superpower in question, and the amount of aid that the superpower had given the rebels or the government. I used these equations:

Political Compatibility =
      Abs(Insurgency Wing − Superpower Wing) − Abs(Government Wing − Superpower Wing)

In this equation, *Insurgency Wing* is the political leaning of the now-victorious rebels, while *Government Wing* is the political proclivity of the *old* government.

Good Aid = Weapons Shipments to Insurgents + (2 * Intervention for Insurgents)

Bad Aid = Weapons Shipments to Government + (2 * Intervention for Government)

Again, *Government* refers to the previous government. The result of all this is the diplomatic affinity of the new government for the superpower in question:

$$\textbf{Diplomatic Affinity} = \frac{\textbf{Political Compatibility}}{\textbf{2}} + \textbf{(8 * (Good Aid − Bad Aid))}$$

This equation covers two areas of affect: political compatibility and past support. It says that the warmth of relations between the superpower and the new government is greater if the new government is politically simpatico with the superpower. In other words, left-wing governments tend to favor the USSR and right-wing governments tend to favor the USA. The second part of the equation expresses the good or bad will generated by past support for, or opposition to, the old insurgency. If you helped the insurgency that won, you will be rewarded with good relations. If you helped the government that lost, then the new government will hate you. In both cases, the intensity of feeling is proportional to the amount of assistance you gave. I multiply by 8 to ensure that history is much more important than politics. This change in diplomatic affinity will, of course, generate a gain or loss of prestige points for both superpowers.

And that is how *Balance of Power* computes the development and results of an insurgency.

HOW ACCURATE IS THIS MODEL?

The system of equations used to model the behavior of an insurgency may strike you as rather brief. One might wonder how so short a set of equations could hope to accurately model so complex a phenomenon as an insurgency. There are two answers to this question, a positive one and a negative one. The positive answer is to point out that the descriptive power of mathematical equations is very high, so even a small set of equations can carry a great deal of meaning. I spent a great deal of time working out, tuning, and polishing the equations in this model.

On the negative side, I must admit that there are many aspects of insurgency that are not properly covered by this model. One is that it doesn't factor in the basic asymmetries of style between right-wing and left-wing governments and insurgencies. *Balance of Power* treats the right wing and the left wing as two faces of the same coin. In the real world, right-wing governments and insurgencies are quite different from their left-wing counterparts. Both tend to be equally bloodthirsty, but their styles can be different. Left-wing insurgencies tend to be more populist in style, while right-wing insurgencies normally obtain more support from the upper classes. Because of this, left-wing insurgencies tend to be more weapons-poor and fighter-rich.

Another shortcoming of the model is its assumption that right-wing governments favor the USA. Although there has been a statistical trend for right-wing governments favoring the USA and left-wing governments favoring the USSR, there is no universal law to this effect. The revolutionary government of the Ayatollah Khomeini is so far to the right that it is downright medieval and yet it cannot be called a friend of the USA. In some cases, American policies have pushed neutralist left-wing governments into the arms of the Soviet Union. The most renowned example of this is Cuba; a strong case has been made that Castro's swing to the USSR came only after it became obvious that severe American opposition to his regime would not abate.

The model also suffers from an overly determinist style by assuming that the progress of an insurgency is a simple matter of military confrontation. No provision is made for special events that can radically alter the course of history. Had Castro died before his victory, it is doubtful that his ragtag army could have held together without the binding power of his personality. The fall of South Vietnam in 1975 is partially attributable to a contradictory set of orders given to a crucial division rushing to stabilize the situation. Had it not been jerked around, South Vietnam might today be in existence.

These are only the most important shortcomings of the model. There are also objections that can be raised against the model from those of strong political persuasions. For example, left-wingers could complain that the model makes no consideration of the element of "populist justice," the notion that most right-wing governments have no legitimacy and that insurgency against these right-wing governments is not merely a military action but an expression of cosmic justice, an act of righteous anger by the oppressed masses against an evil government. On the opposite end of the political spectrum, right-wingers could argue that the model fails to include factors for the perfidious talent that International Communism has developed for subversion of legitimate governments. There is some truth in the claim that left-wing insurgency has been better organized in the 1950s and 1960s than right-wing insurgency, but the renewed interest of the American government in supporting insurgency may be changing all this.

INSURGENCY SCORECARD, 1945-85

Despite all the press that insurgencies generate, insurgency is not a likely way to get ahead in the world. Most insurgencies fail, and rather ignominiously at that. There will always be maniacs crazy enough to take up arms for hopeless causes. In his book, *A Quick and Dirty Guide to War*, James Dunnigan, a historian and Defense Department consultant, lists sixteen separate movements in the United States alone that have spawned political violence in recent years. Each of these could be termed an insurgency, albeit a very low-level insurgency. But that is precisely my point: Most insurgencies never go beyond the occasional bombing. The police round up the perpetrators, shoot or imprison some, and the rest lose heart and give up. Even though every single government in the world faces some degree of insurgency, very few insurgencies ever rise above pointless terrorism. I have not been able to locate data on the total number of terrorist campaigns in the last forty years. This should be no surprise, given the shadowy nature of terrorism.

In the forty years since the end of World War II, there have been some two hundred insurgencies that passed beyond the threshold of terrorism and generated significant numbers of casualties. Of these, about forty (20%) resulted in victories for the insurgents. The government won 80% of the guerrilla and civil wars.

During these forty years, about 42 million casualties (killed, wounded, and missing) have been generated by insurgency. This figure is dominated by the Chinese Civil War of 1945-49, which generated 30 million casualties. Next come the Indochinese (Vietnam, Laos, and Cambodia) wars, which accounted for about 8 million casualties. The remaining 4 million casualties are distributed among the many smaller insurgencies.

MILITARY FACTORS IN INSURGENCY

Insurgency presents special problems for both the rebels and the government. Guerrilla wars are fought in a completely different fashion than conventional wars. A few words on conventional warfare are necessary to bring the special problems of guerrilla war into focus.

The central problem in conventional warfare has always been getting rational human beings to risk their lives in battle. The songs may sing of courage and self-sacrifice, but in the real world of blood and death, normal human beings, if they had their druthers, would much rather drop their weapons and run away. How does the commander prevent such undesirable but rational behavior? The solution has been to create a very strong social group with a powerful grip on the minds of its members. All of the odd customs and values of armies arise from this necessity. The uniforms, the marching about, the flags and traditions—all these things exist to create a strong sense of identification with the group. If that bond is strong enough, the soldier will stay on the battlefield with his group rather than run away as an individual. Of course, this requires that the soldier fight with his group, as an obvious member of the group, rather than as an individual. Concomitant with this approach is the idea of achieving victory by breaking up the social bonds of the opposing army. If you can shock your opponent's soldiers into running away, you can achieve victory far more cheaply than by killing them all. The fact that some bloodshed is avoided with this philosophy is a pleasant secondary result of this form of military efficiency. This thinking has led to the high-density, set-piece battle which has become the standard form of conventional combat.

Leaders of insurgencies quickly learn that their troops cannot fight in this manner, for several reasons. First, set-piece battles tend to favor the side with more and better equipment, and insurgencies are always underequipped. It's insanity to face artillery, tanks, and fighter-bombers with rifles. Second, insurgency fighters tend to be poorly trained, especially when compared with their government opponents. The government can take the time to train its soldiers in safe havens; insurgency soldiers normally get on-the-job training. Third, insurgency forces are normally outnumbered by the government forces. In a set-piece battle, "God favors the side with the bigger battalions."

For all these reasons, insurgency leaders have developed, over the centuries, a different style of warfare, a style that takes best advantage of the insurgency's strengths. The insurgency has two primary advantages, which are motivated soldiers and initiative.

The issue of motivation is often clouded by government propaganda about guerrillas kidnapping young men and pressing them into service, and this probably does happen on occasion, but the bulk of the troops in any insurgency must be highly motivated. It is no great challenge for a guerrilla to slink away from his comrades, with far less fear of retribution than a government soldier might have. Insurgencies rely less on group-identification than on cause-identification. The tremendous advantage of this approach is that it allows the soldiers to fight as individuals rather than as members of the group. This makes possible much lower troop densities during combat. It also makes possible far more diffuse approaches to combat. For example, during the Tet offensive in the Vietnam war, Vietcong fighters engaged government forces deep inside Saigon, Hue, and other major cities. They did not fight their way into the cities as organized units, but rather infiltrated and fought as small groups. Government soldiers could never have been trusted to demonstrate such initiative and drive.

The other advantage that the insurgency holds is initiative. The insurgency leader can decide when, where, and how he will fight. The government commander can only sit and wait for the insurgency commander to make his move. A defense is only as strong as its weakest point; every defense has its weak spots; the insurgency commander need only find them and hit them. In this fashion, an insurgency commander can win one small victory after another, chipping away at the government forces, growing stronger as they grow weaker.

Thus has evolved the classic guerrilla strategy: hit-and-run attacks on government outposts, nuisance raids, and night engagements. The guerrillas keep their forces dispersed, infiltrate government territory, then suddenly concentrate on their target, do their destruction, and immediately disperse again. They never give the government a large target unless they have local, temporary superiority.

Against this strategy, governments have developed their own counterinsurgency techniques. Many experiments have been tried, and many have failed. Perhaps the most spectacular failures arose from the American attempts to win the Vietnam war with firepower. The American forces learned the hard way that hosing down the countryside with quantities of artillery, napalm, and Agent Orange is not an effective way to defeat guerrillas. It appears that victory over a guerrilla force requires a substantial amount of plain old infantry. However, there have been some successful counterinsurgency efforts. The defeat of the Malaysian insurgency is an example often used. The primary government tactic was to deny the insurgents sustenance from the population by securing the villages both militarily and politically. At least, that was attempted; it seems unlikely that so ambitious a goal was truly achieved in entirety. However, the Malaysian insurgency never reached the level of intensity that the Vietnam war reached; perhaps the tactics used can only be successful in low-level insurgencies.

Another counterinsurgency technique is being developed by Soviet forces in Afghanistan. It is a variation on the classic "hammer and anvil" battle tactic, in which a mobile force (the hammer) drives the enemy into a static force (the anvil). The Soviet counterinsurgency version of this tactic is to maintain an extremely mobile force of infantry in helicopters. When the Mujahedeen strike, the airmobile infantry moves quickly to place itself astride the likely escape routes of the guerrillas. Meanwhile, the regular forces pursue the retreating Mujahedeen. When the scheme works, the Mujahedeen stumble into the airmobile infantry and are trapped and destroyed between the hammer and the anvil. The technique's success is founded on the vastly greater mobility of helicopters and the extended visibilities possible in the Afghan terrain.

Insurgency Before the Twentieth Century

We normally think of insurgency as a modern problem made possible only by Soviet largesse with AK-47 assault rifles. Insurgency has been with us as long as governments have. (The very first battle in recorded history, the Battle of Megiddo, was the culmination of an insurrection against Egypt. It gave us the name for what might be the last battle of recorded history: Armageddon.) As long as there has been a government, there has been somebody unhappy with it and willing to raise arms against it. Although the fundamental reason—dissatisfaction with the government's treatment of some group—has never changed, the focus of expression has changed somewhat. In ancient times, insurgency was mostly a tribal matter. The military reach of a powerful government, such as the Babylonian or the Egyptian empires, exceeded their cultural and economic spheres by such a large margin that subject peoples were seldom integrated into the fabric of the empire and bided their time in smouldering resentment until the opportunity for revolt arose. Insurgency in ancient times most often took the form of direct separatism: a town or city would kill the hated imperial tax collectors and close its gates, awaiting the inevitable retribution. Within a few months the imperial army would appear at the gates. Sometimes a magnanimous emperor or terrified populace would initiate a peaceful settlement in which the city got off easily with only an impoverishing tribute and the execution of their leaders. If not, the siege was played out to its bitter end, with either the besieging army departing in defeat, or the city stormed and sacked and the population massacred or enslaved. The Assyrian king Assurnasirpal II records his handling of one insurgent city:

> *While I was staying in the land of Kutmuki, they brought me the word: "The city of Suru of Bit-Halupe has revolted, they have slain Hamatai, their governor, and they have set over them as king Ahiababa, the son of a nobody, whom they have brought from Bit-Adini." With the help of Adad and the great gods who have made great my kingdom, I mobilized my chariots and armies and marched along the bank of the Habur. To the city of Suru of Bit-Halupe I drew near, and the terror of the splendor of Assur, my lord, overwhelmed them. The chief men and the elders of the city, to save their lives, came forth into my presence and embraced my feet. I took Ahiababa captive. In the valor of my heart and with the fury of my weapons I stormed the city. All the rebels I seized and delivered them up. Azu-ilu I set over them as my governor. I flayed all the chief men who had revolted; I cut off the limbs of the officers who had rebelled. I took Ahiababa to Nineveh, I flayed him, and I spread his skin upon the wall of Nineveh.*
>
> (D. D. Luckenbill, *Ancient Records of Assyria and Babylonia*)

An interesting example of the timelessness of the problems of insurgency is the English attempt to subdue Wales during the thirteenth century. The Welsh had little love for English kings and remained in a semi-permanent state of rebellion. The English strategy for pacifying Wales anticipated one American technique in Vietnam by 700 years. They built castles, or, in modern parlance, "strategic hamlets," in which government forces could station themselves in absolute safety against attack. By encouraging (or coercing) the population to settle in towns around the castle, they were able to bring a good portion of the Welsh population under the control of the government. The rebels found themselves driven deeper and deeper into the wilderness, cut off from the population. The insurgency withered and died.

The Renaissance and Reformation brought a series of bloodthirsty insurrections. Although these wars are often characterized as primarily religious in nature, closer examination reveals the same old motivations to throw off oppression. The social makeup of the various Protestant and Catholic armies certainly indicates that these wars were as much social as religious. Most of the early conflicts were little more than peasant revolts dressed up in religious garb.

The Hussite insurgency was typical. Bohemia in the early fifteenth century was infiltrated by Germans who displaced many of the resident Bohemians. The simmering resentment against these invaders exploded into violence when John Huss, a Bohemian heretic, was burned by the Church. The Hussites, as they were called, formed an army under the leadership of

Jan Ziska, a one-eyed old knight, who created the very first tanks by mounting guns on wagons. For twenty years the Hussites fought off the armies sent against them, massacred Germans and Catholics, and maintained a defiant independence. However, their insurgency eventually disintegrated in fratricide and anarchy, and an exhausted population welcomed the return of law and order provided by the Holy Roman Empire.

THE AMERICAN INSURGENCY 1765-83

The American Revolution followed the standard pattern of a successful insurgency, with several unique twists arising from the period and the special military circumstances. The insurgency began in the 1760s with the growing disenchantment of the American colonists towards the mother country. The Stamp Act of 1765 triggered widespread violent resistance; by the standards of *Balance of Power*, this marked the onset of terrorism. It is noteworthy that the actions of the American terrorism phase were mostly directed against tea, property, and other symbols of British oppression rather than taking a bloodier expression. The pressure built up through the late 1760s and into the 1770s with increasingly bolder defiance of the Crown's authority, and the British response was to clamp down harder in a vain effort to assert its authority. The transition from terrorism to guerrilla war came at Bunker Hill in 1775.

The Revolutionary War was not fought with so clean a division between the guerrilla phase and the civil war phase. The primary reason for this lay in the poor accuracy of the musket. Beyond about 50 yards, the concept of aimed fire was meaningless with the musket. Thus, there were only two ways to use a musket in combat: (1) get within 50 yards to deliver aimed fire, a very risky business, or (2) deliver the massed fire of several hundred muskets in the hope of getting a few dozen hits. Conventional European tactics stressed the latter, and the British fought in this manner throughout the war. The problem the Continentals faced was that only a tiny number of their soldiers possessed the marksmanship required for effective guerrilla tactics. Continental tactics were therefore divided between the conventional stand-up battle and the sneak-and-hide tactics used nowadays by guerrillas. They got away with premature resort to conventional combat only because the British forces were far too small for the task they faced.

The French government quickly saw its opportunity to gain some geopolitical advantage and began shipping aid to the American insurgents. Later, they escalated their aid to direct military intervention, and in fact the participation of the French navy was crucial to the final American victory at Yorktown. The Spanish government also provided assistance.

By 1778 the Continentals had gained the upper hand. Operations were conducted in the manner of a conventional civil war; it took three more years to achieve the final British surrender at Yorktown.

INSURGENCY "OSCARS"

If I were giving awards for the most notable insurgencies in history, my awards list would look like this:

BLOODIEST

This is a tie between the Thirty Years' War, an insurgency by North German (Protestant) groups against the (Catholic) Holy Roman Empire in 1618-48, and the Chinese Civil War of 1934-49; each took 30 million lives.

LONGEST

The Basque separatist insurgency. The Basques have fought the Carthaginians, the Romans, the Visigoths, the Arabs, and the Spanish, only achieving success for a few hundred years during the Dark Ages. One would think they would have given up (or won) by now.

MOST CONFUSED

The Russian Civil War of 1918-22. The original government was overthrown in a coup, its replacement was overthrown six months later in another coup, and then a reactionary insurgency developed against the new (Red) government. We had the Reds (communists), the Whites (royalists and republicans) contesting the form that the new government of the

Russian empire would take. Then we had the nationalists of the various subject peoples, trying to break away from the Russian empire: the Poles, Czechs, Finns, Estonians, Latvians, Lithuanians, Ukranians, Cossacks, and Siberians. Then we had the interventions from France, Germany, Britain, the United States, and Japan, half-heartedly pursuing a number of diverse opportunistic goals. The war rambled along for a while, generating millions of casualties, until it drowned in its own blood. The Reds did not so much win as simply outlast everybody else.

MOST FUTILE

A tough choice here, as there are so many worthy contestants, but the Jewish Revolt of 70 A.D. takes the cake for the utter futility of a small, unorganized people challenging the Roman Empire at the height of its power. The brutal truth was that the revolt against the Romans was doomed from the start. Under normal circumstances the majority of the population would have realized this and refrained from making matters worse. But the intensity of Jewish national and religious feelings drove the population into furious resistance, with consequent catastrophic casualties—perhaps a million people died in the fighting, and nothing was gained.

BEST STAGE-MANAGEMENT

Castro's Cuban insurgency. The military reality was this: Castro's guerrillas skulked about impotently in the remote mountains, assiduously avoiding combat and generally losing when they did get into combat. The Batista regime was disintegrating under its own venality. At the moment it disintegrated, Castro came down from the mountains and declared himself the victor in the "heroic struggle." The fact that the 30,000-man Cuban army fell apart after sustaining only 200 killed is a pretty good indication of how little combat there really was.

BEST SUPPORTING ROLE

The American assistance to the South Vietnamese government during its losing battle. Never has a supporting actor so completely supplanted the leading man.

BEST SPECIAL EFFECTS

Again, the American effort in Vietnam takes the prize for its liberal use of smart bombs, napalm, Agent Orange, and a whole host of other ingenious devices.

BEST DAVID-AND-GOLIATH SCENE

The Neuchatel affair. In 1856, republicans in the city of Neuchatel in southern Germany seized power and repudiated the suzerainty of Prussia over their city. They instead chose to federate with Switzerland. Prussia was at the time a major European power. It seemed to all that the Prussian elephant would simply step on the Neuchatel fly. However, the French and British, wary of Prussian power, sided with the insurgents and pressured Prussia into accepting an unfavorable settlement.

BEST INSURGENCY-RELATED NAMES

Top honors go to Stenka Razin, ill-fated leader of a sixteenth-century Cossack revolt against Moscow. He was taken to Moscow in a cage and executed. Honorable mention goes to Sendero Luminoso, the bloodthirsty "Shining Path" of Peru, for having the courage to shun trite acronyms involving "People," "Liberation," and "Fronts."

COUPS D'ETAT

A fruit of a successful insurgency is a revolution: a sudden and violent change in the basic makeup of a government. There is a less violent way of effecting governmental change. The most general term for this alternative is "change of executive." This is a rather unwieldy and academic term, so *Balance of Power* lumps all such changes of power under the more familiar label *Coups.* This chapter will explore the nature of coups d'etat and describe how *Balance of Power* handles them.

A coup produces a change of executive. The old leader is thrown out and a new leader is installed in his place. The middle and lower levels of government are left intact; only the top is changed. There are two variations on this: the "regular change of executive" and the "irregular change of executive." The first uses recognized legal procedures such as an election to remove an existing leader; the second uses less formal procedures such as a bullet through the head.

The difference between a coup and a revolution lies primarily in the intensity of violence used. A revolution is a simple contest of military power between two implacable opponents. Each side believes that defeat is tantamount to death. Each side believes strongly in the fundamental truth and rightness of its position, and each side believes the other side to be evil. The wide gap separating the two sides in an insurgency makes negotiated solutions almost impossible. Most insurgencies are fought to the bitter end. The loser does not admit defeat until defeat (and gun barrels) is staring him in the face.

Coups are normally resolved with less violence. Many coups are bloodless; even the most violent coups seldom involve more than a few hundred casualties. Moreover, bloodshed is seldom an intended side effect of a coup. It arises only when the coup falters and factions start to shoot. Allthough massive violence is the prime strategy of any insurgency, it is the first unravelling of a coup.

Another difference between a coup and an insurgency lies in the time scale of their evolution. An insurgency takes years to develop and grow; some insurgencies have dragged on for decades, and even the fastest take several years. A coup, by contrast, spends perhaps some months in planning and hours in execution. Even the longest-running coup conspiracies seldom last more than a few years.

A third difference between coups and revolutions is that revolutions normally generate dramatic changes in society, while coups seldom do so. In some cases, a coup generates almost no policy changes whatsoever; the only issue in question is the identity of the man in charge. In a very few cases, coups generate the kind of sweeping changes that we normally associate with revolutions. There is a reason for the less dramatic nature of the changes normally associated with coups. Any party that espouses dramatic changes—of any kind—will certainly frighten a large group of people. The fear of the entrenched and the opportunistic excitement of the deprived are seldom made compatible without recourse to violence.

A SPECTRUM OF VIOLENCE

There are many types of coups, or at least many political phenomena that I have chosen to lump into the broad category of coups. They can be sorted and categorized on the basis of a single major variable: the amount of violence associated with the coup. I shall start my discussion at the most violent end of this spectrum and work my way toward the more peaceful coups.

VIOLENT MILITARY COUPS

The most violent coups develop from attempts by factions within the military to sieze power. Sometimes this can be accomplished without much fighting, but if a substantial base of loyal supporters of the existing regime can be mobilized before the plotters' seizure of power is consolidated, heavy fighting will ensue. The recent fighting in Yemen was of this nature, but it represented an extreme in which the units supporting the two sides were determined to achieve success, so the fighting proved to be long and bloody. The coup in Yemen demonstrates just how deadly modern weaponry can be when used in straight, stand-up fighting instead of the more protracted tactics of guerrilla warfare.

Far more typical of the military coup was the attempted coup in Thailand of 1985. Several military units converged on the presidential palace. Loyal military units were rushed to the rescue. After several tense hours and a few warning shots, the rebellious units were convinced that their actions had not sparked a general revolt, and laid down their arms. There were only a few casualties.

PALACE COUPS

A variation on the military coup is the palace coup. This is an attempt to keep casualties down by focusing military power directly on the president and his immediate staff. The instigators show up at the presidential palace with a few soldiers and put a gun to the president's head. If all goes well, he gives in. Perhaps they simply shoot everybody and take over. Two problems make the palace coup more difficult these days.

First, in the more rough 'n' ready nations, presidents have had the good sense to keep a powerful guard on the premises at all times. It gets harder and harder to pull off a simple invasion of the presidential palace. The Soviets found this out to their dismay when they assisted their fraternal brothers in Afghanistan. Their intention had been to take a few soldiers up to the presidential palace and put a bullet through the head of Hafizullah Amin, the Afghan president. Unfortunately, they did not bargain on the stiff defense that his guards put up, or their considerable number. A furious battle raged for nearly a day, with Amin himself manning the barricades. When it was over, there were quite a few casualties, not the least of which was the Soviet story that this was a simple political reshuffling with Soviet fraternal assistance.

The second problem with the palace coup is that, in the more genteel nations, assassinating the president doesn't make you the new president; it makes you only an assassin. You suddenly find the entire nation—most importantly, the entire military—lined up against you. Oops!

NONVIOLENT MILITARY COUPS

The next step in our spectrum of coups is the nonviolent military coup. The idea here is to use the military to demonstrate power and intimidate your opponents while still avoiding violence. The attempted coup against Hitler in July, 1944, was of such a nature. The conspirators planted a bomb to kill Hitler and then moved to arrest his supporters in Berlin. Their only violent act was the bombing itself; otherwise, their coup was executed with pistols, guards, and a great deal of bluff. They failed, partially because several crucial military commanders refused to acknowledge the legitimacy of any leadership that was founded on naked military power. In effect, the conspirators failed because the German generals were too civilized to accept something as brutal as a military coup. How's that for irony?

Often a military coup is a simple matter of the generals losing confidence in the civilian government and showing up at the presidential palace with a few tanks and announcing that the civilian government is being replaced by a military junta. Ostensibly, the junta will deal with the current emergency and then hold elections as soon as the situation has calmed enough to enable elections.

Perhaps one of the most civilized military coups in history was the attempted coup in Spain a few years ago. A Spanish colonel showed up in the Cortes (the Spanish equivalent of our Congress) with a few soldiers, shot a few rounds into the ceiling, and announced that the fledgling democracy was suspended by the military. He expected other elements of the military to fall in with his initiative. Spain held its breath: What would the military do? At this moment, King Juan Carlos donned his military uniform and appeared on television, denouncing this "criminal act" and throwing the full weight of his prestige behind the democracy. That did it. Generals telephoned in their pledges of loyalty, and the entire affair was reduced to a nut case with a pistol in the Cortes. He surrendered and is now in jail. This affair demonstrates the immense value of a constitutional monarch. By remaining above politics, the monarch retains the confidence of all the people, regardless of their ideology. When the chips are down, and democratic fractiousness threatens to tear society apart, the monarch can step in and throw the weight of his prestige behind the forces of law and order. That is precisely what King Juan Carlos did. On that day, he earned his pay for many a year. We Americans, who swear loyalty to a Constitution, have some difficulty understanding the system, but we cannot deny that it works.

POPULAR REVOLTS

The next form of coup is the popular revolt. Popular resentment against the government boils over into street demonstrations which become riots. If enough people are angry with the goverment, they quickly realize one of the fundamental truths of the world: that no government can function without the consent of the people. No military or police force, no matter how large or powerful, can maintain control over a population against its will. Having smarted under the whip for too long, the population goes wild in an orgy of rioting. This demonstrates that the government has lost all ability to govern. Let's face it, if you can't even keep peace in the streets, you don't have a functioning government. The only option is to fold up the tent and let a new government take over. This is how the people of Haiti overthrew the hated Baby Doc Duvalier. The Haitians overcame their fear of the Tontons Macoutes, Duvalier's murderous secret police, and overthrew his government. A similar set of circumstances led to the fall of the Shah of Iran, again in spite of Savak, the Shah's secret police. The Polish communist government of Edward Gierek was overthrown a similar manner in 1970, despite the array of repressive measures available to a communist state.

These examples of successful popular revolts are the exceptions, not the rule. Civil unrest is the norm in many nations of the world and it boils into the streets with depressing frequency. In all three of the above-cited cases (Haiti, Iran, and Poland), the leadership refused to acknowledge the seriousness of the situation until it was too late. The reason for such a callous attitude is the frequency of civil disorder and its usual lack of issue. Most of the time, the police crack down and the crowds disperse after venting their rage. There have been some 10,000 riots in the last forty years; about 100, or 1% of these, yielded a change of executive. Little wonder that political leaders seldom see civil disorder as a threat to their jobs.

POLITICAL COUPS

The next form of coup is the purely political coup. The Soviet Union and many communist states rely heavily on this form of governmental renewal. They are able to do so because one of the fundamental disciplines of any communist state is the maintenance of absolute party control over the military. Thus, the prospect of a coup involving the military is much less likely in communist states. Since there are also no true elections, the only means for replacing an ineffective leader is the political coup. This is normally carried out through a series of complex political intrigues, the goal of which is to create a new consensus against the current leadership and in favor of some new leader. The danger of this lies in the difficulty of hiding these intrigues from the leader and thwarting his subsequent countermoves. The 1964 ouster of Nikita Khrushchev illustrates the process. A series of bad harvests and economic failures set the stage for the coup. Khrushchev foolishly took a vacation in the south, giving the conspirators the opportunity to work openly in Moscow. Khrushchev threw away his last chance at retaining power when he failed to respond to warnings telephoned him by his loyalists. By the time he was ready to act, it was too late: the Brezhnev-Kosygin party had consolidated its political position within the Party hierarchy and Khrushchev's ouster was complete.

INSTITUTIONALIZED "COUPS"

Here we pass into the forms of coup that are institutionalized. These are primarily the preserve of the Western democracies. These nations have developed a more organized and less disruptive way of sweeping out the cobwebs. Most nations in the West use a parliamentary democracy with a coalition government that exists only so long as it enjoys the confidence of the Parliament. Once it loses a formal vote of confidence, it must dissolve itself and organize a new coalition. The system used by the United States involves regularly scheduled elections to replace the government executives.

FACTORS THAT CONTRIBUTE TO COUPS

Almost anything can contribute to the dissatisfaction that leads up to a coup. The Spanish colonel who raided the Cortes believed that democracy was rotting the moral core of Spain, and that military leadership was necessary to put Spain back in order. The Argentine generals who took over in the 1970s did so because they felt that the civilian government was impotent against the left-wing terrorism that was crippling the nation. Personal ambition can play a large part in coups; Napoleon's coup against the Revolutionary government was not an expression of any particular social grievance, but merely the bold stroke of an ambitious man grasping for power.

ECONOMICS

The single largest factor in coups, though, is simple economics. When people's stomachs grumble loudly enough, governments fall. Runaway inflation has been a common motivating factor in coups. In American politics, the performance of the economy plays a large role in every national election. A strong economy bodes well for the incumbents; a weak one gives the challengers a big boost. The real issue is not so much the total GNP as it is GNP growth. For example, the rapidly growing nations of Eastern Asia (South Korea, Singapore, Taiwan, and Japan) have enjoyed political stability as well. Their neighbors who have grown more slowly (Philippines, Thailand, and Malaysia) have experienced more political instability.

For the purposes of *Balance of Power* I have chosen to concentrate not on GNP growth, but instead on the growth of consumer spending per capita. Consumer spending is the amount of money that is left over to spend on the direct well-being of the population after military spending and investment is taken out of the GNP. It includes such things as food, clothing, and housing. Consumer spending is the only means by which the average citizen actually experiences the GNP. The government can announce all sorts of wonderful statistics, but such propaganda has far less credibility than the amount of bread on the table. Note that in some countries, the GNP is growing more slowly than the population, so that GNP per capita, and hence consumer spending per capita, is falling even though the GNP is growing.

THE ROLE OF THE SUPERPOWERS

The superpowers are unable to prevent or control coups around the globe, but they are able to create and influence them. A variety of schemes are available to the superpower; their effect is referred to as *destabilization*. The foreign espionage services (the CIA and the KGB) are the normal vehicles for destabilization. Efforts can be kept fairly sanitary, such as simply providing funds for the opponents of the regime. Henry Kissinger asserts that this was the extent of the Nixon administration's efforts to destabilize the Allende regime in Chile. Superpowers can go much further than this if they wish. They can provide assistance to the more determined opponents of the regime. The KGB has been implicated in a number of assassinations associated with political intrigues in a variety of countries. The strongest influence that a superpower can exert comes in the moments of crisis. At these times a superpower with domestic influence can encourage one side or the other. The United States, for example, played a role in encouraging the coup against Diem, leader of South Vietnam, in 1963. Similarly, the American refusal to support the Shah of Iran in the last days of his rule was a major factor in his decision to throw in the towel.

ECONOMIC AID

Superpowers do have some options to support a regime. The most effective of these is simple economic aid. Inasmuch as poor economic performance is a major contributor to the unrest that leads up to coups, any aid that improves the economy will strengthen the regime. Unfortunately, there are many limits on the value of foreign aid. In the first place, foreign aid must actually reach its destination; many Third World nations are so hopelessly tangled in corruption that only a fraction of the foreign aid they receive reaches its intended destination. Second, political considerations often result in the foreign aid being used in a manner not likely to achieve the maximum improvement in the GNP. The vanity of the recipient-nation's leadership, or the dictates of the giver, may result in the construction of a grandiloquent but useless dam, road, or factory.

Results of a Coup

A coup has two primary aftereffects. The first and most obvious is the replacement of the old executive with a new one. This can mean very little or it can mean a great deal. Many African coups merely replace one tribal dictator with another. On the other hand, the popular coup

73

against the Shah of Iran led to radical changes in Iranian society.

The second aftereffect of a coup occurs only with irregular changes of executive. Such events erode the society's confidence in, and respect for, its institutions. If Petty Tyrant #1 can march into the presidential palace, shoot the president, take the reins of power, and get away with it, why can't Petty Tyrant #2 do the same? And then how about Petty Tyrants #3, #4, and so on in an unending series?

Coups in Balance of Power

Balance of Power treats coups in a very simple-minded fashion: economic performance is the primary factor that determines the generation of coups. A secondary factor is the political leaning of the government: Extremist governments of either stripe are accorded a small amount of resistance to coups. Because economic performance plays so large a role in the determination of coups, I shall also present a summary of the economics computations used in *Balance of Power*. The first equations are:

Consumer Pressure = (20 − Government Popularity) ∗ 10
IF Consumer Pressure < 1 THEN Consumer Pressure = 1

Investment Pressure = (80 − Investment Fraction) ∗ 2
IF Investment Pressure < 1 THEN Investment Pressure = 1

Consumer Pressure is the degree to which the government feels compelled to increase consumer spending at the expense of the other two main sectors of the economy (investment and military spending). *Government Popularity* in *Balance of Power* normally falls between 1 and 20, with a value of 20 indicating a very popular government. These equations say that the government feels more pressure to increase consumer spending when its popularity falls.

Investment Pressure is the degree to which the government feels compelled to increase investment spending. This is normally a small pressure. The investment fraction is the fraction of the total GNP that is invested in the form of new roads, schools, factories, and the like. In *Balance of Power,* it is measured not from 0% to 100%, as one might expect, but from 0 to 256; this range is better suited to the peculiar arithmetic considerations of a digital computer using 16-bit words. A typical investment fraction would be 40, corresponding to about about 15% of GNP.

The third economic factor used in calculating the incidence of coups is *Military Pressure*, computed with a more complex formula:

Military Pressure =
> **Square Root of Insurgency Strength Ratio + Probability of Finlandizing to the USA + Probability of Finlandizing to the USSR**

IF Military Pressure < 1 THEN Military Pressure = 1

Now we're getting messy. *Military Pressure* is, as you might expect, the amount of pressure the government feels to increase its military budget. Three factors contribute to *Military Pressure.* First comes the square root of the strength ratio between the insurgency and the government. If this number is large, then the insurgency is large and powerful, and the government had better strengthen its army. The second and third numbers are the "Finlandization probabilities" for each of the two superpowers. They measure the degree to which the government feels vulnerable to, and threatened by, each of the superpowers. Military spending is one way a government can increase its sense of security in such circumstances. One might argue that no minor power could seriously believe that it could defend itself against a superpower, but such is not the case. The Nicaraguan government of Daniel Ortega believes that by arming itself to the teeth, it will make the cost in blood of an American invasion too high for American planners to contemplate.

These three forms of pressure on the GNP budget are then brought together to determine how the GNP will be allocated:

Total Pressure = Consumer Pressure + Investment Pressure + Military Pressure

Fractional Pot = 0

IF Consumer Fraction > 16 THEN Consumer Fraction =
Consumer Fraction − 8 AND Fractional Pot = Fractional Pot + 8

IF Investment Fraction > 16 THEN Investment Fraction =
Investment Fraction − 8 AND Fractional Pot = Fractional Pot + 8

IF Military Fraction > 16 THEN Military Fraction =
Military Fraction − 8 AND Fractional Pot = Fractional Pot + 8

The effect of these strange statements is to create a "Fractional Pot" of GNP fractions that we are then going to reallocate between the three primary sectors of the economy. The purpose of the IF-statements is to protect sectors that are so tiny (less than 16 parts in 256, or 6%) that they must be held inviolate. But any sector that has more than 6% of the total GNP must throw in 8 units of its fractional part of the GNP into the common pot, from which new GNP portions will be allocated:

$$\text{Investment Fraction} = \text{Investment Fraction} + \frac{\text{Investment Pressure} * \text{Fractional Pot}}{\text{Total Pressure}}$$

$$\text{Military Fraction} = \text{Military Fraction} + \frac{\text{Military Pressure} * \text{Fractional Pot}}{\text{Total Pressure}}$$

$$\text{Consumer Fraction} = 255 - \text{Military Fraction} - \text{Investment Fraction}$$

These equations say that each sector of the economy gets a portion of the fractional pot in proportion to the amount of pressure that it generated. The purpose of all this code is to simulate, in a very crude fashion, the type of decision-making that goes on in every society in the world. Leaders must always allocate limited funds to meet insatiable demands. By expressing this problem through the concept of pressure, I was able to get a very rough approximation of the decision-making process.

This is not to say that my equations assume that the division of the GNP between the military, investment, and consumer sectors is decided upon by the government. The equations deal only in the pressures operating on the society and how those pressures are resolved in a distribution among the three primary sectors (military, consumer, and investment). Whether that resolution is determined by a government minister, the marketplace, or by powerful bankers, is not the concern of the model. It is true that the model makes some strong assumptions about how different societies will react to military threats and the need for investment. In the absence of usable data on national differences of this kind, I opted for a "one size fits all" model.

With the GNP divided between the sectors, we are ready to calculate the change in consumer spending:

$$\textbf{Old Consumer Spending Per Capita} = \frac{\textbf{255*(Consumer Spending)}}{\textbf{Population}}$$

$$\textbf{Virtual GNP} = \textbf{GNP} + \textbf{Economic Aid From Superpowers}$$

$$\textbf{GNP} = \textbf{GNP} + \frac{\textbf{(Virtual GNP * 2 * (Investment Fraction} - \textbf{30))}}{\textbf{1000}}$$

The first equation is simple enough—it directly calculates the consumer spending per capita. The second is a little strange. It creates a "virtual GNP" that will be used for computational purposes but is not identical to the true GNP. Much of it is lost in the third equation, which makes the GNP grow by the portion of the economy that is invested in the future. Notice, though, that any investment fraction less than 30 (about 12% of the GNP) will result in negative growth of the economy. This is based on some simple empirical data I obtained on growth rates of GNPs and investment fractions. I plotted them against each other and found a roughly linear relationship with slope and intercept corresponding to the coefficients that are used in the third equation. This, apparently, measures the average depreciation of capital assets. In other words, if you don't invest at least 12% of your GNP each year, your roads, factories, schools, and so on will wear out faster than you can replace them, and your GNP will diminish.

Now we are ready to calculate the new consumer spending with the equation:

$$\text{New Consumer Spending Per Capita} = \frac{\text{Consumer Fraction} * \text{Virtual GNP}}{\text{Population}}$$

And at last we are ready to calculate the percentage by which consumer spending per capita has grown:

$$\text{Improvement} = \frac{100*(\text{New Consumer Spending Per Capita} - \text{Old Consumer Spending Per Capita})}{\text{Old Consumer Spending Per Capita}}$$

Now we are able to calculate this year's government popularity. The equation is simply:

$$\text{Government Popularity} = \text{Government Popularity} + \text{Improvement} + \frac{\text{Abs(Government Wing)}}{64} - 3$$

Now I must explain each of the terms in this last formula. The first term, *Government Popularity*, simply says that the government starts off with the popularity it had last year and works from there. This takes into account the idea of loyalty: People who like the government will not turn on it overnight without strong incentives. In short, the government does not start with a clean slate each year; a good job last year will generate popular goodwill that will carry over into the next year.

The second term, *Improvement*, is the critically important economic performance term. If the government achieved an improvement in consumer spending per capita, the average citizen's life is better and the government's popularity is increased. If, on the other hand, consumer spending per capita went down, then improvement will be a negative number and the government's popularity will fall.

The third term, using *Government Wing*, presents one of the most debatable assertions in the entire model. It declares that a government's popularity will increase in proportion to its radical-ness. Remember, extreme left-wing governments will have *Government Wing* equal to up to -128, while governments with an extremely right-wing orientation will have *Government Wing* equal to $+128$, and *Government Wing* for centrist governments will be 0. Thus, the radical governments of either wing will get a one-point popularity bonus solely because they are so radical. I added this term to reflect two forces: the tendency of radical governments to suppress dissent, and the divisiveness that so often cripples centrist governments. Fortunately, the effect is small, only appearing as a single point for truly extremist governments.

The last term is simple in appearance but carries a great deal of baggage in the way of assumptions. I subtract 3 from the government's popularity. This we might call the "natural expectation of the masses." The idea behind this term is that people expect economic growth. In fact, people expect a 3% growth rate in consumer spending per capita. If the government achieves that, they are satisfied. Not pleased, mind you, just satisfied. If, however, the government falls short of the expected 3% growth rate, then they are dissatisfied, even if the growth was still positive. How did I determine this magic number? Did I spend hours in the library compiling economic statistics and cross-checking them against expressions of political discontent? No! I arrived at it by experiment. I found that 2% was so low that people were always happy with their governments and there were never any coups in the game. That was too boring. On the other hand, 4% made it impossible for any government to survive the game, so that was too high. That left 3% as the happy medium that generated enough coups to make life interesting but not hopeless. If only the real world were as manageable as a game design . . . .

So now we have calculated the new popularity of the government. The next task is to determine if a coup is triggered. This is simplicity itself:

IF Government Popularity < (USA Destabilization + USSR Destabilization) THEN Trigger a Coup

Normally, neither superpower will be engaging in destabilization, so this IF-statement boils down to the simple question, Is *Government Popularity* less than zero? If, however, one or both superpowers is indeed carrying out a program of destabilization, it will express itself as a positive number between 1 and 5, corresponding to the 5 levels of destabilization allowed in the window brought up by selecting Destabilization from the Make Policy menu. Thus, in the unlikely event that both superpowers were exerting maximum destabilization effort, the government would fall if its popuarity were less than 10.

If a coup takes place, a number of changes result. As with the insurgency, the *Government Wing* is reversed, so that the left-wingers are replaced by right-wingers, and vice versa. The new

81

government starts off with a fresh load of popularity, because people everywhere let their hopes exceed their judgment.

On the other hand, the government's resistance to insurgency is weakened; its soldiers don't fight as well when they don't know for whom they are fighting.

The other result of a coup involves the government's relationship to the superpowers:

Change in Relations =

   (Abs(Insurgency Wing − Government Wing of Superpower) −

   Abs (Government Wing − Government Wing of Superpower)) div 2

The effect of this equation is to measure the "ideological distance" that the new government moved toward or away from the ideological stance of the superpower. If it moved closer to the superpower, then diplomatic relations between the two countries are improved; conversely, if it moved farther away, then diplomatic relations are worsened.

And that is how the details of coups are handled in *Balance of Power*.

SCORECARD: COUPS, 1948-77

The *World Handbook of Political and Social Indicators* (Taylor and Jodice 1983) presents a compendium of political events during the thirty years from 1948 to 1977. The following is a digest of some of the more interesting tidbits gleaned from that source.

The authors define four types of events that fall within the purview of this chapter: *regular executive transfers, irregular executive transfers, unsuccessful regular executive transfers,* and *unsuccessful irregular executive transfers.* An irregular executive transfer is the "removal and replacement of the incumbent national executive outside the conventional procedures for transferring formal power." A regular executive transfer is the same process carried out through legal or conventional procedures. Thus, we normally think of an irregular executive transfer as a coup, but in the world of *Balance of Power,* any form of executive transfer is treated as a coup.

The term *unsuccessful regular executive transfer* may perplex readers unfamiliar with parliamentary democracy. In such a system, a government (actually, not the entire government but the executive echelon of the government) operates only with the confidence of the Parliament. If for any reason the government is unable to survive a vote of confidence in the Parliament, the government is declared dissolved, which means that a new government must be formed. During the period of forming a new government, an out-of-power faction may make a legal attempt to form a majority government. If this attempt fails, it is considered to be an unsuccessful regular executive transfer.

The authors report a total of 238 irregular executive transfers during their sample period versus 304 unsuccessful irregular executive transfers. In other words, about 44% of all coup attempts were successful. That's better than twice the success rate of insurgency. Regular executive transfers are even more impressive: 1645 successful regular executive transfers against 409 unsuccessful ones. That's a success rate of 80%!

There is an interesting and reassuring relationship here. The most violent and brutal form of political change—insurgency—has obtained a success rate in the last forty years of only 20%; the next most brutal form, the irregular executive transfer, achieved a 44% success rate, while the most civilized form of political change, the regular executive transfer, enjoyed a success rate of 80%. Those who fear the world is descending into barbarism take note.

For optimists and pessimists alike, another aspect of the data is bad news: there has been no clear secular trend in the incidence of coups, successful or unsuccessful. Year in and year out, coups seem to march along with depressing regularity, neither increasing nor decreasing in frequency.

Some countries have set records for the numbers of coups they have undergone. Top honors are shared by Bolivia, with 18 unsuccessful coups and 6 successful ones, and

Syria, with 12 unsuccessful coups and 12 successful ones. Conspirators take note! Syria is a much friendlier place for a coup attempt than Bolivia. Until Hafiz Assad took over in 1970, Syria was one of the most politically active nations in the world. In addition to its 24 irregular executive transfers (successful and unsuccessful), Syria has had more regular executive transfers (48) than any other nation in the world. It ranks sixth in unsuccessful regular executive transfers (with 24), and, believe it or not, 16th in national elections—with 15—the same number as the United States has had in the same period. Hafiz Assad changed all that and brought "stability" to Syrian politics. This is not so bad as it might seem: During the sample period, before Hassad assumed power, Syria suffered nearly 2,000 deaths from political violence and 28 assassinations.

In the field of national elections, the Swiss hold the record with 43 elections, with France coming in second with 26. Would you believe that Algeria has had more national elections (18) than the United States (15)? Or that the Soviet Union has had more national elections (7) than Hong Kong (1)?

It should come as no surprise that France and Italy are the record-holders for unsuccessful regular executive transfers, with 61 and 41 respectively. However, most of the French instabilities arose during the fifties, and most of the Italian turbulence came in the sixties.

Those who like to think of Western democracies as the proper role-models for governmental change for the Third World nations will cringe upon discovering that, of the top ten countries in the category of regular executive transfers, only Greece can be called a Western democracy. The other countries with the most regular executive transfers are mostly in the Middle East. France is 11th with 29 regular executive changes. And what do the Soviet Union, Bulgaria, Afghanistan, East Germany, Czechoslovakia, Poland, China, Rumania, Kuwait, Uganda, Malawi, and the Philippines have in common? They *all* had more regular executive transfers than the United States, which has had only 6 such events in the thirty-year period. How are we to interpret this? One might argue that the infrequency of American regular executive transfers is an indication of stability, not lawlessness. Certainly one cannot claim that the number of elections or regular executive transfers is a measure of the quality of democracy.

THE HISTORY OF COUPS

The history of coups is not as long as that of insurgency. The early civilizations weren't civilized enough to accept the notion that power could be transferred without violence. Throughout much of history, the transfer of power from one executive to another was a violent and bloody process that took a large toll of all bystanders, innocent or otherwise. Power struggles of this nature were so disruptive that most civilizations developed a deep-seated fear of them. From this fear arose a rich collection of values about the means by which a king should be replaced with minimal disruption to society. The exclamation, "Long live the king!" was not an altruistic expression of good wishes for the royalty; the longer the king lived, the lower the chance of a bloody dynastic struggle. Similarly, the birth of a male heir to the throne was always received by the commoners with great joy. The eldest male heir was universally regarded as having an unimpeachable claim to the throne upon the death of his father; such certainty of succession greatly reduced the likelihood of dynastic wars upon the death of the father. On the other hand, people dreaded the existence of multiple male heirs: Additional heirs injected an element of uncertainty into the succession that was all too easily exploited by ambitious siblings to generate bloody battles. The Turks came to accept the notion that royal siblings must ruthlessly murder each other until one emerged victorious.

The first truly modern coups of which I am aware come from Roman history. Julius Caesar did not pull off the first military coup, but his crossing of the Rubicon and subsequent entry into Rome is certainly the most famous of early coups. Moreover, it set precedence and created the model for future Roman transfers of power.

The Dark Ages were too primitive a time to allow much in the way of coup activity. Here is how King Sigibert of the Franks was removed from office in 575 A.D.:

> *Two young men who had been suborned by Queen Frede-gund then came up to Sigibert, carrying strong knives, which are commonly called scramasaxes, and which they had smeared with poison. They pretended that they had something to discuss with him, but they struck him on both sides. He gave a loud cry and fell to the ground. He died soon afterwards.*
>
> (Lewis Thorpe, trans., *History of the Franks: Gregory of Tours*)

The history of these times is twisted chronicle of murder and wild anarchy. The concept of a coup just doesn't seem to work in this environment. It was about as appropriate as raising a point of parliamentary procedure in a barroom brawl.

By the time of William the Conqueror, things had progressed far enough that we can once again talk about transfers of executive power as opposed to bloody free-for-alls. The next seven hundred years were dominated by the development of the king-state relationship. Coups revolved around dynastic considerations. The developing rules for dynastic succession worked most of the time, but when they failed, a major civil war such as the English Wars of the Roses ensued.

The central rules of dynastic succession might be summarized as follows: When a king dies, the throne goes to his eldest legitimate son. If that son is not yet old enough to rule (generally less than 18 years old), then a regent is chosen to rule in the name of the child-king until he reaches his majority. The regent is usually a close relative, such as an uncle. If no son is available, things get sticky. If a daughter is available, the crown might be given to her. The fact that the daughter is married could be a positive or a negative factor. If no acceptable child is available, then perhaps a brother of the dead king can be given the crown. Failing in all these options, the society is forced to fall back on weak claims to the throne, of which there are always many. Distant relatives come out of the woodwork to lay their claim. Foreign royalty steps forward with obscure claims. (William the Conquerer had a tenuous claim to the throne of England, which claim was the pretext for his invasion.) The ambiguity of all these claims insures that the matter will be resolved by that most terrible arbiter of men's fates: Mars.

The French Revolution signaled the end of dynastic change of executive. With the collapse of the old order came new ways of making governmental change. Times of change are also times of instability. In the early years of the United States of America, Aaron Burr led an effort that could be called an attempted coup. Europe experienced popular uprisings in 1830,

1848, and 1870. It seems that nations need a generation or two of democracy before their governments acquire a resistance to coups. Thus, French democracy did not shake free of its vulnerability until the early twentieth century, and German democracy began in 1920 and did not stabilize until 1960.

THE PHILIPPINE COUP, FEBRUARY, 1986

The most recent and dramatic coup was the removal of President Ferdinand Marcos by Corazon Aquino. The turbulent events surrounding this coup underscore the complexity and ambiguity inherent in all coup activity. Many people have difficulty deciding whether it was a revolution or a coup. According to the terms of *Balance of Power*, it was definitely a coup, but the sequence of events was quite complicated. Let's walk through them.

Marcos initiated events with his announcement of a snap election. He obviously thought that he would easily win this election, but as the campaign progressed it became apparent that considerable electoral fraud would be necessary to win. The election that should have confirmed his leadership only served to disprove it. The large incidence of fraud convinced many Filipinos that Marcos had, in truth, lost. The coup proper began in the days immediately after the election. As more and more stories of fraud spread, large groups of disaffected citizens demonstrated their anger in the streets. This kept the heat on. It created a new social contract between Filipinos, a contract of opposition to the Marcos regime which was now commonly perceived as illegitimate. Most importantly, it smoked out Marcos and stampeded him into making the crucial mistake that the opposition needed.

On February 22, Marcos had a group of soldiers arrested in the belief that they were part of a plot against him. They were not, but the action alarmed the man who turned out to be the key player: Defense Minister Juan Ponce Enrile. Enrile had helped establish the "Reform the Armed Forces Movement," a group of about 100 professional military men who were disenchanted with the growing politicization of the Filipino armed forces. Although the group had never contemplated sedition, its very existence during such sensitive times could easily have been construed as a threat to Marcos, so when Enrile heard of the arrests he concluded that he was also a target. In effect, the arrests flushed Enrile out of a quiet opposition and into a stance of open defiance. He resigned his position as Defense Minister, recruited General Fidel Ramos, and with the other members of the group set up a defensive position not far from the presidential palace.

This was open rebellion. It was the first clear, continued, steady act of outright defiance of Marcos' authority. It served as the vital focal point, the locus of crystallization for the popular revolt against Marcos. Any coup or rebellion of this nature always faces a crisis of crystallization: Who will take the first step? Who will make himself the locus of discontent and the target for retribution? Many coups fail because no hero (or martyr) can be found to place himself in the crosshairs of the rebellion. The irony is that Marcos forced Enrile's hand and precipitated him into that regime-shattering move.

The crystallization was rapid. Thousands upon thousands of Filipinos showed up at the defensive compound to protect the rebels from military action with the shield of their own vulnerability. Other military units began to rally around the standard they had raised. The complete disintegration of Marcos' authority took less than 72 hours. By Tuesday evening, February 25, Marcos had fled.

The American role in all this was greater than most people, imbued with images of sign-waving Filipinos, would believe possible. The Americans intervened diplomatically at several crucial points. The first American contribution was the steady pressure on the Marcos regime that goaded him into calling elections to demonstrate his mandate. The second contribution was the monitoring of the elections that helped expose considerable fraud and, more importantly, add credibility to the many other accusations of fraud. Two absolutely crucial moves were made during the rebellion crisis. On Monday, February 24th, General Fabian Ver, loyal to Marcos, prepared a military attack against the rebels. The White House announced that American military aid to the Philippines would be cut off if such an attack took place. More pointedly, the National Security Council advised General Ver that he would forfeit any hope of American protection if he ordered the attack. The attack was canceled. The second crucial move was made by U.S. Senator Paul Laxalt in telephone conversations with Marcos. Laxalt advised Marcos to give up the hopeless struggle. This was the last blow for Marcos, who trusted Laxalt and knew that his words reflected the views of President Reagan. Marcos had lost the support of his people and now he had lost the support of the United States. He began making arrangements to leave.

The Philippine coup involved a complex mix of many elements. There was a democratic election, an election that, in the eyes of the Philippine people, should have awarded victory to Corazon Aquino. There was a popular nonviolent revolt against Marcos, but this by itself might not have toppled him. There was also a military rebellion, but it resulted in almost no fighting and no deaths. There was also the diplomatic intervention of the United States. Taken singly, none of these forces could have toppled Marcos so quickly. Taken together, they swept him out of office. Was it a coup, a popular rebellion, a revolution, or a military revolt? It's hard to say—none of these terms capture the complex events of February 1986. *Balance of Power* takes the whole confusing mess and packs it into a neat little box labeled "coup d'etat."

Coups Around the World

Every culture has its rituals associated with the transfer of power from one executive to another. Because this transfer is so vital to the stability of society, the entire process is invested with a great deal of ritual. For example, here in the United States we have the presidential nominating convention with its straw hats, its signs and banners, and its arcane voting process always prefaced with, "The great state of _____ casts its votes for . . . ."

In Latin America, one of the procedures is called the *pronunciamento*. This is a military coup carried out by the entire officer corps against the government. It begins with a polling of officers for their views, then a commitment by all to each other. With these preliminaries out of the way, the coup can be carried out with a clear conscience.

A German version of the military coup is called a *putsch*. Hitler tried one in 1923 and succeeded only in killing 19 people and landing himself in jail. The German generals tried one against Hitler in 1944 and succeeded only in getting several hundred of their faction murdered. A variety of other putsches took place in the early 1920s; none was successful.

THE ROLE OF THE MILITARY IN COUPS

Armies are for fighting wars, right? That may be true in this country, but in most countries of the world, the army exists almost exclusively for dealing with internal enemies. Very few armies of this world have any capability for operating beyond their national boundaries. Of all the armies of the world, only the armed forces of the USA and the USSR have any significant capability for operations outside their base territories. For example, the United States Marines are the world's largest expeditionary force (designed for operations anywhere in the world) with nearly 200,000 troops, while the analogous Soviet force has only 12,000 troops. And these are the forces of the superpowers!

In most Third World countries, the primary function of the army is to protect the government from challenges to its authority. The problem is, what happens when the challenge comes from within the army?

This delicate problem first arose a couple of thousand years ago. Julius Caesar crossed the Rubicon and took control of the Roman government. Actually, the fact that Caesar crossed the Rubicon wasn't half so important as the fact that several legions crossed the Rubicon with him. Caesar was able to get away with it because the troops were more loyal to him than to the government. In a single stroke, Caesar destroyed the already shaky Roman democracy and set the pattern for Roman changes of executive. With the passage of time, the precedent that Caesar set was expanded. Within a few hundred years, the Praetorian Guards had become the arbiter of Roman succession. Any emperor who lost their favor, they killed. At first, new emperors were chosen with some consideration for the sensibilities of the other factions of the Roman government, but with time even the pretense of legality was dispensed with.

Ever since then, political leaders have struggled with the problem of controlling their military forces. A variety of solutions have been tried. During the Dark Ages, the military and the government had no problems getting along because they were the same thing. Military power defined political power; the king was simply the most powerful warlord. Later, the military was controlled by an aristocracy that swore loyalty to the king. This system worked most of the time, but there were occasional lapses, such as the Decembrist plot against the Tsar of Russia in 1825.

The United States and the Soviet Union have developed the most effective solution to the problem. The American solution is to inculcate a profound reverence among the officers for the Constitution. This can only work with a highly educated officer corps and a stable democracy, but since such conditions obtain in this society, the strategy is effective. There is no credible possibility of a military coup in the United States.

The Soviet solution is radically different. The armed forces are under close supervision by the party. Every military unit has two commanders: its normal military commander, and its *politrabochiy,* a political officer who is a member of the Communist Party and whose loyalty is to the Party, not the Army. There are politrabochiy at all levels of the armed forces, right down to the company level. The politrabochiy is not trained as an officer and is promoted by the Party, not the Army. Ostensibly, the function of the politrabochiy is to provide political indoctrination to the men in the unit. His real purpose is to keep an eye on the unit to make certain that any anti-Party grumblings are dealt with quickly. His authority is superior to that of the commander of the unit.

Few Third World nations have the right conditions to use either the American or the Soviet technique. Therefore, they must accept the likelihood that the troops will come out of the barracks and throw out the current leaders. Only about 10% of all post-war coup attempts have not involved the military in some fashion, and the success rate of coups not involving the military is only about 60% that of coups involving the military.

FOUR SYSTEMS

It can be instructive to compare the experience of different political systems in replacing their chief executives during periods of relative calm. I have chosen four systems to compare: Ancient Rome, Medieval England, Imperial Russia, and the United States of America. For each system I have chosen a period free from foreign invasion or other external forces that exerted a major influence on questions of succession.

The Roman period extends from 27 B.C. to 192 A.D., a duration of 219 years. During this time, 17 emperors reigned. Of these, 8 died in political violence. The average reign was 13 years.

The English period begins in 1377 and ends in 1603, for a total of 226 years. This was a difficult time for England, for it endured the Hundred Years' War, the Wars of the Roses, a major peasants' revolt, and some religious strife associated with the formation of the new Anglican Church. Nevertheless, during this period, 13 monarchs reigned, and only 2 died in political violence. The average monarch reigned for 17 years.

The Russian period comprises the first 212 years of the Romanov dynasty, beginning in 1613 and ending in 1825. This period saw 14 Tsars, 3 of whom died or were forcibly removed from office. The average member of this dynasty held power for 15 years.

The American period covers the entirety of our history as an independent state, 210 years. During this time, we have had 40 Presidents, 3 of whom have died in political violence. Most presidents enjoyed only a single term in office; the average incumbency was only 5½ years in duration.

What is surprising about these four systems is their similarity. Except for the Romans, each system suffered two or three violent removals from office. Except for the Americans, the average reign in each system was about 15 years in duration. Considering that this small collection spans two thousand years of history and four very different political systems and cultures, these similarities are striking.

FINLANDIZATION

alance of Power uses a term that is unfamiliar to many Americans: *Finlandization.* Finlandization is an expression of simple anticipation and common sense. The process takes place whenever a polity realizes that its military position is hopeless, and therefore attempts to make some sort of accommodation with superior forces. Although the idealist in each of us may feel disgust at such unprincipled behavior, there can be little doubt that it has saved more lives and prevented more bloodshed than any other form of diplomacy.

HISTORY OF FINLANDIZATION

This term refers to the experience of Finland at the end of World War II. The original story goes back to the end of World War I. Of all the many peoples yearning to break free from the Russian empire at the end of that war, only the Finns and the Poles were successful. The Russians resented the independence of these two nations but were too weak to do anything about it—at least, for a few years. The Western powers, primarily France and Britain, guaranteed the independence of both Poland and Finland. The very first act of World War II was the German invasion of Poland, with the Russians joining in after thirty days to take over the eastern half of Poland. With Poland out of the way and the British and French fighting the Germans, the Soviets were free to invade Finland. In December, 1939, they attacked. The Finnish forces were outnumbered but fought with great skill, inflicting tremendous losses on the lumbering Soviet columns. Eventually superior Soviet numbers prevailed and the Finns were forced to cede large portions of their land to the Soviets in a dictated peace settlement.

Then came the German invasion of Russia in 1941. The Finns joined in the German attack so that they might recover their lost lands. When the war began to turn against the Germans, the Finns realized their mistake and began to make peace overtures to the Russians. Rebuffed by the Soviets and facing invasion, they turned to the Western Allies. Their pleas fell on deaf ears; they were still allied with Nazi Germany and could not expect to receive protection. Realizing the hopelessness of their situation, the Finns had to accept a humiliating surrender which only preserved their existence as a nation.

Since the end of World War II, Finland has pursued a foreign policy extremely deferential to Soviet interests. While nominally a sovereign state with a neutralist foreign policy, Finland is in practice very much under the sway of the Soviet Union. For example, during Soviet naval maneuvers in the White Sea, a Soviet cruise missile went out of control and flew into Finnish airspace. One would have expected a diplomatic protest and angry denunciations of Soviet callousness. Instead, the Finns quietly collected the pieces of the cruise missile and returned them to the Soviet Union.

Although the term *Finlandization* dates from 1945, the process has been taking place since earliest times. Thus, Julius Caesar reports in *The Conquest of Gaul*:

> *These various operations had brought about a state of peace throughout Gaul, and the natives were so much impressed by the accounts of the campaigns which reached them, that the tribes living beyond the Rhine sent envoys to Caesar promising to give hostages and obey his commands ....*

Acts of Finlandization don't occupy the prominent place in the history books that the famous battles have; the battles get all the press coverage because they are the turning points that conveniently mark the waxing and waning of a nation's fortunes. Yet, in many cases the real significance of a battle comes from the acts of Finlandization toward the victor that the battle induces from previously reluctant minor powers. For example, William the Conqueror may have won the Battle of Hastings in 1066, but that victory did not by itself hand over all of England to his forces. There remained considerable military forces on English soil capable of effectively resisting Norman arms. The psychological effect of the battle was to convince all onlookers that William had established decisive superiority, and the remaining Anglo-Saxon nobility made their obeisance to William.

Finlandization can also take place in reverse. A major power that has established suzerainty over a variety of minor powers can suddenly find its position under threat if its prestige or power appears to collapse. The total collapse of the Napoleonic hegemony after his defeat in Russia is a classic example of such an unraveling. By 1811, Napoleon had established hegemony over Austria-Hungary, Prussia, Denmark, Italy, and the Low Countries. Then came the 1812 invasion of Russia and his disastrous defeat. Within six months his subject nations had all rebelled against him. In 1813 came the Battle of Nations at Liepzig, and just about everybody who was anybody was there with an army against Napoleon. Liepzig, not Waterloo, marked the real destruction of Napoleon's power.

METHODS OF ENCOURAGING FINLANDIZATION

Finlandization is an act of anticipation; it is possible to take the anticipation one step further and anticipate the act of Finlandization. In other words, not only can a minor power anticipate its likely defeat at the hands of a major power, but a major power can also anticipate the intimidating effects of its behavior on minor powers. This creates a whole panoply of behavior calculated to maximize or minimize the intimidation of minor powers, such as terror, punitive expeditions, or military demonstrations.

DESTRUCTION AND TERROR

The most extreme example of such deliberate intimidation was the behavior of Ghengis Khan in the first decades of the thirteenth century. The Mongol armies adopted a deliberate policy of terror. When they invested a city, they gave the inhabitants a simple choice: surrender immediately or suffer complete destruction later. Cities that surrendered were forced to give up tribute and hostages, but were allowed to continue their existence. Cities that offered any resistance were obliterated and all inhabitants massacred. The effect of this terror campaign was to create a paralyzing fear of Mongol armies. The stratagem was effective but based on a hideous destruction of human life.

Such brutal techniques have contemporary analogies in the Soviet treatment of rebellious satellites. The Soviet invasions of Hungary, Czechoslovakia, East Germany, Poland, and Afghanistan were carried out with a vindictive ferocity exceeding that necessary to restore order. Although the primary goal of these military actions was the reestablishment of Soviet control of the satellite, a secondary effect was to make clear to the other satellites that any rebellious behavior would be met with naked and overwhelming force. The point has not been lost on the Eastern European nations. During the Polish troubles of the early 1980s, all parties—Solidarity, the government, and the general population—lived in dread fear that the Soviets would lose patience with the efforts of the Polish government and put a stop to Solidarity's efforts in its own way: with a brutal invasion.

PUNITIVE EXPEDITIONS

One step down from the deliberate use of terror is the so-called "punitive expedition." This is a limited military operation against a weak nation whose purpose is to shoot up the countryside in a fashion calculated to impress the natives with the power of the military forces arrayed against them. The European nations used such techniques against China in the 1880s, keeping it in chaos and subservient to Western trading interests. The phrase "gunboat diplomacy" dates from this period and captures the style perfectly. The American actions against Libya in 1986 also fall into this category of behavior.

NONVIOLENT DEMONSTRATIONS OF POWER

At the next lower level of intimidation, we have the nonviolent demonstration of military power. Commodore Perry's expedition to Japan in the 1850s falls into this category. The Commodore was sent to open up trade with Japan. The warships he brought were merely for protection, but of course, only a fool could fail to see how big and powerful they looked. The Japanese took the hint and acceded to the good Commodore's "suggestions." Within a few years the Japanese began to develop a Western-style navy of their own.

Similarly, the American demonstration of naval power against Nicaragua in 1982 was nonviolent in character yet managed to convey a truly menacing message to the Nicaraguan leadership. The Navy sailed around offshore, looking mean and hungry. While Commodore Perry's use of intimidation was successful, the American use of intimidation against Nicaragua had no apparent success.

Intimidations of this nature need not be pointed directly at their intended victims. For example, the American invasion of Grenada in 1982 could be regarded as, among other things, an attempted indirect intimidation of Nicaragua.

DIPLOMATIC INTIMIDATION

From here we pass out of the sphere of military intimidation and into more diplomatic channels of intimidation. Here, the trick is to say the magic words that will convince your victim that he is in deep trouble and had better come around to your way of thinking. Adolf Hitler was a master of such techniques; his was the remarkable achievement of successfully conquering Austria and Czechoslovakia using only brutal browbeating, without a shot being fired.

COUNTERMEASURES

Some nations may not wish a major power's attempted intimidation to succeed, and they have a variety of countermeasures available to them. The object of the attempted intimidation might prominently display its military power to demonstrate its resolve to fight. The Sandinista government of Nicaragua has responded to American attempts at intimidation with extensive military displays meant to show Nicaraguan determination to fight. In ancient times, leaders desiring to blunt the intimidating threats of enemy ambassadors would execute those ambassadors. The practice might seem barbaric at first glance; its real purpose was to present the citizens with a fait accompli. Murdering ambassadors guaranteed awful retribution for the entire polity associated with so heinous an act, and so served to win the enthusiastic cooperation of all citizens in the endangered kingdom.

A major power wishing to blunt the intimidations of a rival major power can bolster the resistance of a minor power with assurances of support. This is the basis for treaties of friendship and mutual defense treaties. Indeed, throughout history, the vast majority of treaties between nations took the basic form of a powerful nation undertaking to defend a less powerful nation. By guaranteeing the weaker nation's security, the stronger nation bound the weaker nation to it more tightly and effectively reduced its sovereignty.

The problem with this technique is that it can be carried out with so much anticipation that it can drag nations into disaster. The genesis of World War I provides the perfect example of how the anticipation and counter-anticipation used in such mutual security treaties can lead to failure. Europe had known peace for forty-five years; during that time it had stabilized a set of delicately balanced power relationships. A web of mutual security pacts was strung across the whole European continent. Germany, wary of Russian pressures on Austria-Hungary, had signed a security treaty with that aging empire. France, fearful of burgeoning German power, signed a security treaty with Russia. Britain was also worried about German naval programs. Thus, when Austria-Hungary declared war on Serbia, it triggered a chain of similar declarations. Russia entered the war in protection of Serbia; Germany declared war on Russia because of its treaty obligations to Austria-Hungary; France thereupon declared war on Germany; and Britain soon entered the fight.

*T*HE ROLE OF PRESTIGE OR "FACE"

World leaders are often castigated for going to great lengths to "save face." The impression one gets is that these are vain old men who freely sacrifice the lives of young soldiers to preserve their sense of dignity and "save face." As it happens, there really is a functional significance to the role of prestige, and the sacrifice of human life in pursuit of prestige is not so monstrous as it first appears.

Prestige confers two benefits in the world of geopolitics: one for friends, one for enemies. High prestige tends to demoralize or intimidate unfriendly nations. They will be less likely to challenge the nation that enjoys high prestige. If a major power's prestige falls, unfriendly nations will be emboldened to take action against the now-weakened power. This process can mushroom as each act of defiance encourages still others, as Napoleon learned the hard way.

Even more important is the effect of prestige, or its loss, on a major power's friends. Every major power collects around it a covey of client states, each of which accepts the risks of association with that power in return for the protection it provides. Their willingness to continue the association with the major power is contingent upon their confidence in that major power, which in turn is closely tied to its prestige. For example, in 413 B.C., Athenian prestige was shattered by twin defeats. An Athenian army and navy at Syracuse, in Sicily, were annihilated, and a Spartan force captured Deceleia, a strategic town not far from Athens. The twin defeats triggered mass defections from the confederacy that Athens had built. Her allies abadoned her, her subject cities refused further tribute, and even the slaves in the mines revolted. Prestige can build empires bloodlessly, but such empires collapse with the loss of that prestige.

The same considerations played a major role in the long agony of American disengagement from Vietnam. As early as 1969, a consensus had been reached that the fundamental American goal was eventual disengagement. Yet, American participation in the war continued on for four more long years, withdrawal being stymied by the problem of minimizing the loss of prestige that a unilateral withdrawal would entail. Henry Kissinger, discussing the problem of North Vietnamese violations of the 1973 treaty, wrote:

> *We were convinced that the impact on international stability and on America's readiness to defend free peoples would be catastrophic if we treated a solemn agreement as unconditional surrender and simply walked away from it. And events were to prove us right.*
>
> *(Years of Upheaval)*

Roughly 20,000 American lives were expended while this problem was wrestled with.

FINLANDIZATION IN BALANCE OF POWER

Finlandization in *Balance of Power* presents a simplified version of the considerations described in this chapter. The first task of the Finlandization routines is to determine the extent of military vulnerability of the subject nation. This must be compared with the amount of military threat imposed by each of the superpowers. If a superpower can project a believable military threat against a small nation, and that nation believes that the superpower might actually carry out its threat, then the small nation will Finlandize.

The procedures begin by defining the *Military Excess* as the military superiority of the government over the local insurgency:

Military Excess = Military Power of Government − Military Power of Insurgency

This is the amount of military power that the government has available for defense from outside forces such as a superpower. You will recall from Chapter 2 that the military power values of the government and the insurgency are calculated from the number of soldiers and weapons available to each.

The program then calculates the amount of military power that each superpower can project against the minor country:

$$\text{Projectable Power} = \frac{\text{Intervenable Troops} * \text{Military Power of Superpower}}{\text{Total Troops of Superpower}}$$

In this equation, *Intervenable Troops* represents the total number of troops that can be placed into the minor country by the superpower. This is itself is a complex consideration. A superpower may have a great many troops, but its ability to place them in any country in the world is severely constrained. Unless it is invited in by the government, the superpower will have great difficulty with the logistical problems associated with moving large numbers of troops into a hostile environment. In *Balance of Power*, this problem is handled in a very simple fashion. If the superpower is contiguous with the minor country, then it can apply the full measure of its power—all of its troops—against the minor country. If it is not contiguous with the minor country, then its ability to send in troops is based on the existence of a third country, contiguous with the minor country in question, in which the superpower has based troops in support of the government. The presumption is that such military installations create logistical facilities which can support the infiltration of military forces across the border. The number of superpower troops that can be used against the victim minor country is then equal to the number of superpower troops based in the neighboring country. For example, the American troops based in Honduras are there primarily to put pressure on the Nicaraguans. Finally, if there is no contiguous country in which the superpower has stationed troops, then the superpower can still send up to 5,000 men. This force represents the small mobile forces that both superpowers keep for just such purposes. It is the basis for our time-honored slogan, "Send in the Marines!"

The *Military Power of Superpower* is computed in the same way that military power is computed for the minor countries; it is a function of the number of troops and weapons available to the superpower. The *Total Troops of Superpower* is just that—the total number of men under arms, and is calculated from the total population of the country.

With projectable power calculated, the next step is to determine the amount of military support that the minor power can expect from the *other* superpower. This is based on three factors: the military power of that other superpower, its treaty obligations to the minor country, and its record of integrity in honoring such treaty obligations. These are expressed as an equation:

$$\text{Expected Military Support} = \frac{\text{Treaty Obligation} * \text{Military Power of Superpower} * \text{Integrity}}{16384}$$

To expand on these terms: *Treaty Obligation* is the extent to which a superpower is committed to defend the minor country. It is dependent on the level of treaty support between the two countries. In *Balance of Power* there are six levels of treaties, ranging from "no treaty" to "nuclear defense treaty." These treaties create obligations using the following table:

Treaty Type	Amount of Obligation
No relations	0
Diplomatic relations	16
Trade relations	32
Military bases	64
Conventional defense	96
Nuclear defense	128

The other strange term in the equation is *Integrity*, which may surprise the reader. After all, one would not expect to see a variable in a computer program called *Integrity*. There is certainly something unsettling about the thought of computing integrity. This is one of our finest and most cherished virtues, a hallmark of our moral sensibilities. There is something both presumptuous and outrageous about attempting to reduce so noble a concept as integrity to a few ciphers in a computer program. It borders on sacrilege.

My reply to these reservations is to claim that the attempt to quantify a concept in no way demeans it. If something exists—that is, if it is real—then its very existence implies a set of numbers that characterize its properties. That set may be very large, or very difficult to determine, but they do exist, and making a stab at getting a few of them is not sacrilege. We all know (or should know) that a person's IQ does not define his or her mental ability; it is only a score on a test and the only thing it tells us with certainty about that person is the ability to answer silly questions about odd geometric shapes. We generalize that number to make statements about the person's native intelligence, but we realize that we are on very thin ice when we do so. And skating on thin ice is not tantamount to sacrilege. So, on with the computation of integrity.

In *Balance of Power, Integrity* is a number between 0 and 128. A lying, scheming, no-good varmint gets an integrity rating of 0; a truly honest man gets a rating of 128. Each superpower starts off with an initial integrity rating of 128. This is admittedly a ridiculously generous assessment, but I felt that each player should have the opportunity to make his own evil. A superpower's integrity is changed whenever a government falls. When this happens, each superpower's integrity is decreased in proportion to the strength of the treaty commitment the superpower had made to the newly-fallen government. For example, when the insurgents win a revolution, or there is a coup d'etat, the following equation is applied for each superpower:

$$\text{Integrity} = \frac{\text{Integrity} * (128 - \text{Obligation})}{128}$$

Thus, if the USA has a nuclear defense treaty (*Obligation* = 128) with a nation whose government falls, the *Integrity* of the USA will fall to 0. Ouch! If it had only a military bases treaty (*Obligation* = 64), then its *Integrity* would be cut in half.

You may notice that this equation will always *reduce* a superpower's *Integrity*. That's a cynical view of international relations. To correct for this problem, I threw in the following formula and had it executed once each turn:

$$\text{Integrity} = \text{Integrity} + 5$$

IF Integrity > 127 THEN Integrity = 127

This formula says, "Look, kid, you keep your nose clean, your reputation will get better each year slowly." You may ask, "Why did you choose the number 5? Why not 4, or 6, or 20?" Good question! When I wrote that equation, and realized that I had to choose a number, I leaned back in my chair, stared at the ceiling, closed my eyes, squeezed on the eyelids, and watched the dancing phosphenes form the numeral 5.

Does it bother you to realize that some aspects of this game were chosen so arbitrarily? If so, consider the problem of choosing the correct value for the equation. How quickly does a nation's reputation recover from damage? How could anybody possibly measure this? In other words, there is simply no rational way to arrive at an estimate for this number. There are no books in which to look it up, no scholarly studies, nothing of which I am aware. This leaves only two possibilities: fabricate a number or abandon the concept. I chose to fabricate the number.

Of course, my concoction is not completely without rational basis. We can easily whittle the possible choices down to a number between 1 and 50. For example, any number less than 0 would imply that one's reputation grows *worse* with time, even if you do nothing wrong. That's not the way the world works! The number 0 implies that, with no activity on your own part, your reputation does not change. But this formula is meant to reflect the aphorism that "Time heals all wounds," so we cannot accept a value of 0. On the upper end, any value larger than 50 would imply that one could commit the most heinous crimes and enjoy the absolute confidence and respect of the world only two or three years later. The world's memory isn't *that* short. This does suggest the means to narrow down the range of possibilities. How many years should go by before a country's reputation recovers? A value of 20 would imply complete recovery of reputation in only six years. That seems a little quick to me.

So we know that our final value should be between 1 and 20. But which value to choose? At this point, we have exhausted the possibility of easy solutions. There is simply no reliable way to choose, say, 5 over 6. A good case can be made for any value in this range. And, if it is possible to make a good case for any value, then there is no harm done by choosing one value from this range arbitrarily. If I am unable to determine whether a value of 5 is better than a value of 6, how would a player ever be able to tell that something is wrong with the game if indeed the value I chose was incorrect vis-à-vis the real world? What is the meaning of "incorrectness" when nobody is able to discern it?

The last bit in the equation that needs explanation is the divisor, 16384. Its purpose is to scale the value back down to its proper range. Since *Integrity* and *Obligation* both range between 0 and 128, if both are at full value, they will multiply together to produce 16384. By dividing by this figure, we bring the *Expected Military Support* back to its proper range.

Now that we have calculated the military support that the minor country can expect from the other superpower, we calculate its total defensive strength:

Defense Strength = Military Excess + Expected Military Support

This number will be used to calculate the *Finlandization Probability*—the likelihood that the minor country will Finlandize to the superpower in question. The magic equation is:

Finlandization Probability =

$$\frac{\textbf{(Adventurousness} - \textbf{Diplomatic Affinity)} \ast \textbf{Projectable Power} \ast \textbf{(Pressure} + \textbf{4)}}{\textbf{Defensive Power}}$$

Now to explain the new terms. *Adventurousness* is the demonstrated proclivity of the superpower to engage in reckless military actions. It is calculated from the following formula:

Adventurousness =

Pugnacity + Nastiness − *other* Superpower's Pugnacity − Military Fraction + 32

Oh, no! And you thought I went too far with measuring integrity! Now I'm using *Pugnacity* and (gasp!) **Nastiness** ?!?! Where do I get those? *Pugnacity* is a number between 0 and 128 that is initialized at the beginning of the game to a value of about 64. I say "about" because a small random number is added to make sure that each game plays slightly differently. Also, the Soviet Union gets a pugnacity rating 32 points higher than the USA, although for me recent events in Libya call into question the wisdom of this assessment. I will not go into the many details of the calculation of pugnacity and nastiness. Instead, I will say that a superpower's pugnacity is increased whenever it engages in aggressive behavior, and decreased when it engages in more conciliatory behavior (such as backing down in a crisis). *Nastiness* is a term that applies to the overall situation rather than to any single superpower.

Nastiness is increased by military interventions and crises. It is decreased only by the balm of time. The effect of these two terms is to create a mood to the game. Players who pursue confrontational strategies will increase their own pugnacity and the game's nastiness. Executed properly, such a ruthless strategy will encourage weak nations to Finlandize to the player. But minor slips can cause the other superpower's pugnacity to increase and your own pugnacity to fall as you find yourself backing down too many times in crises.

The other new term in the equation is *Pressure*. This is the amount of diplomatic pressure that the superpower is applying to the minor country, ranging from 0 to 5. This makes it possible for a superpower to induce Finlandization in a minor country that is on the brink. Note that adding 4 to the value of the pressure insures that zero pressure does not mean zero chance of Finlandization.

When all these terms are put together, we get a number for the Finlandization probability. If this number exceeds 127, then we say that the country has Finlandized to the superpower in question. This triggers a number of changes. First, the victim changes its political alignment to become more like that of the superpower:

New Government Wing =

$$\text{Old Government Wing} + \frac{(\text{Superpower Government Wing} - \text{Old Government Wing})}{4}$$

You will recall from Chapter 2 that *Government Wing* is the position of the government on the ideological spectrum, with far left countries having a *Government Wing* of -127 and far right countries having a value of +127.

The Finlandizing minor country also changes its diplomatic affinity towards the superpower; it decides to be nicer to the superpower:

New Diplomatic Affinity = Old Diplomatic Affinity + 32

Old Diplomatic Affinity is the previous value of *Diplomatic Affinity;* the degree of good feeling between the two governments. This is an important equation because this is what gives the player prestige points. Prestige points are what win the game for the player, and they are generated by the extent to which the player's country is held in esteem by the countries of the world, weighted by their military power.

And that is how Finlandization is computed within *Balance of Power.*

Europe, NATO, AND "NEUTRALIZATION"

For the last forty years, the central strategic problem of American planners has been the protection of Europe. At first this was strictly a military problem, the response to which was NATO, but as time went on the problem assumed more delicate dimensions. The Soviets have realized that a simple invasion of Western Europe would be prohibitively dangerous. However, they have not missed the opportunity to play on European fears. The basic strategy is to steadily harp on the enormous damage that would be created by a European war. The intermediate-range nuclear weapons were one expression of this policy. Their purpose was to drive home to the Europeans the fact that Europe could easily become a nuclear battlefield in the event of any conflict. It may surprise some Americans, accustomed to living in the shadow of the Bomb, that the awful significance of nuclear weapons had not quite penetrated the European political consciousness. The Europeans had always thought that a nuclear war would be fought over their heads. They would see the missiles flying overhead, and hear the distant detonations, but would themselves face "only" the depredations of conventional warfare. All through the late seventies and early eighties the significance of the new Soviet weapons tormented the European public, igniting a storm of protest. The Soviet strategy had the desired effect on a portion of the European public. These people reasoned that the cost of alliance with the United States was too high if it carried the responsibility of being targeted by Soviet intermediate-range missiles. They felt that the superpower competition was not their doing, and they were not willing to risk their homelands in the pursuit of that competition. They therefore argued that a much safer course would be to distance themselves from the United States and take a more neutralist course. Security would come from the same neutrality that Sweden, Austria, and Switzerland had chosen.

This was precisely the course that the Soviet Union desired. If Western Europe could be coaxed into neutrality, NATO would be dismantled and there would exist no effective counter to Soviet power in Europe. A blatant invasion would still be too risky, but strong pressure could slowly be applied to edge the nations of Western Europe into increasingly more accommodating positions. Eventual Finlandization would be the outcome. And the results for the Soviet Union would be spectacular. With Western Europe under Soviet sway, the Soviet sphere would certainly outweigh the American sphere. World hegemony would be conceivable.

This line of thinking, or variations on it, has certainly generated many nightmares for American planners. For example, Henry Kissinger, discussing the European diplomatic overtures to the Soviet Union in the early 1970s, wrote:

> *A European race to Moscow might sooner or later represent the first steps toward the possible Finlandization of*

Europe—in the sense that loosened political ties to America could not forever exclude the security field . . . .

(Years of Upheaval)

Fortunately, the nightmare lost momentum. The Soviet intermediate range missiles were countered by American cruise missiles. There was much opposition to these cruise missiles at first, but ultimately they were accepted by their host countries. NATO held together. But the Soviet effort to drive a wedge between Europe and the United States will continue.

Variations on Finlandization

There have been many variations on Finlandization throughout history. It seems that statesmen have been very creative in coming up with alternatives to sovereignty or subjugation. Modern Finlandization is a very genteel matter. The victim defers to the superpower in matters of foreign policy, and generally makes nice to the superpower. However, there are many variations on this basic theme. Among them:

THE UNWILLING ALLY

This has been a fairly common theme throughout history. The little country would really rather be left alone, but the big country needs the assistance of its army to bolster its own military power. Thus, the Soviet Union has imposed the Warsaw Pact on its Eastern European satellites. Napoleon did the same thing when he invaded Russia in 1812; of the 600,000 men in the Grand Army, less than half were French. The bulk of the Army was filled by Germans, Italians, Dutch, Belgians, and Poles who were "fulfilling their duties as brothers of the Revolution." The effectiveness of such shanghied allies became apparent during the retreat from Moscow, when the Army melted away. Many of the soldiers died of the cold or were killed by Cossacks, but many others simply abandoned Napoleon.

Ancient Athens used exactly the same procedure to build the Athenian hegemony of the Golden Age of Greece. The Athenian league was, on paper, an alliance of equals with Athens playing the role of first among equals. In practice, Athenian behavior was closer to that of superpower dictating to allies who dared not contradict their master.

THE VASSAL

This was a feudal concept originating in German tribal structures. Society was organized on simple hierarchical lines. Every man had his superior, or liegelord, as well as his inferiors, or vassals. The vassal owed service to the liege; in return, the liege was obligated to provide protection to the vassal. The concept was applied from the very bottom of society right up to the very top, and so was applied to international relations. A weak leader might seek the protection of a strong one by offering himself as vassal. More commonly, a strong leader might use whatever pretext he could concoct to assert liege rights over a weak leader. It is misleading to compare this directly with the modern concept of Finlandization, for all society was organized along such liege/vassal lines, so the creation of a new liege-vassal relationship could be called an act of annexation or an act of Finlandization.

TRIBUTE

This technique was used throughout ancient history. A weak nation would send regular payments to a powerful one. The system was remarkably similar to the concept of "protection money" that we see used by street gangs. The victim makes regular payments to the stronger party. In return, the victim obtains two benefits: the victim is not molested by the strong party, and the strong party acknowledges a vague responsibility to protect the victim from other molesters. This responsibility is not strong enough to allow a victim to demand action when it is molested; it is rather a matter of the strong party protecting its territory from incursions by other molesters.

BUYING OFF

This was a variation on tribute, normally used by powerful nations with pesky nomads. The powerful nation is not actually weaker than the nomads, but does not have the resources to eliminate them. Instead of maintaining extensive military forces to protect the frontiers from their raids, the powerful nation simply sends them a payment every year. The payment does not constitute tribute and no subordinate status is implied. It is just a simple buying off of a nuisance. For example, the Eastern Roman Empire used this technique to keep the Huns off its back. Even at the height of their power under Attila, the Huns did not constitute a serious threat to Constantinople, but they had beaten several Roman armies and could wreak great damage in the Balkan provinces, so Emperor Leo agreed to pay an annual tribute of 2,100 pounds of gold.

CRISES

A crisis, in the context of this book, is a diplomatic confrontation that carries a serious risk of war. The crisis is a recent historical development first made possible by the telegraph. Before the invention of the telegraph, news traveled at the speed of a fast horseman. Capitals were separated by days of time, and diplomacy moved at an appropriately leisurely pace. Kings and diplomats felt no need to hurry their deliberations; there was always time to sleep on the matter before a decision need be made. Moreover, the slow speed of news made it impossible to react to many events. All too often, by the time a diplomat learned of a developing problem, he knew that the matter had probably been already resolved. Finally, leaders were forced to rely heavily on their ambassadors to carry out discussions. These ambassadors, skilled in the use of diplomatic language, could rephrase the less-than-tactful recriminations of their leaders and keep the flow of diplomatic intercourse moving along smoothly.

The telegraph dramatically changed the operation of diplomacy by making it possible for leaders to communicate directly with each other on a time scale of hours. In the last decades of the nineteenth century, the newfangled telegraph played an uncertain role in statecraft, but experience refined its utility. The modern crisis, after some rocky early days, had established its basic form and substance by the turn of this century.

*I*NITIATING EVENT

Every crisis is triggered by some salient event. It might be a diplomatic move, military action, or even a personal affront. For example, the Franco-Prussian War of 1870 was triggered by the infamous Ems telegram. Chancellor Bismarck of Prussia created this supposedly internal memorandum and then surreptitiously leaked it to the press; it contained slanders against the French nation. The outrage this generated in France made war inevitable.

Sometimes the initiating event appears to be innocuous to most bystanders, but the relationship between the two parties is so strained that even minor matters become issues of state. Thus, in the months before the outbreak of World War I, a crisis was nearly precipitated over the sending of a German military legation to Turkey. It is quite common for nations to trade military legations, and the German legation was in no way meant to be provocative. Yet Russia was extremely sensitive about Turkey and nearly initiated a crisis over the German legation. Similarly, the Germans were quite incensed during the summer months of 1914 by the treatment accorded their ambassador in Paris. They felt that he was being excluded from the French social scene, and were sure that this was proof of warlike French intentions. The possibility that the ambassador was personally obnoxious did not occur to them.

The most colorful initiating event was the famous Defenestration of Prague in 1618. Tensions had been running high between local Protestants and the Catholic Emperor over a variety of issues. On May 23, one of the Protestant leaders invaded Hradschin Castle in Prague at the head of a mob. They found two of the Emperor's governors in a second-floor room. They threw them out the window (Latin *de*: out of, *fenester*: window). Unfortunately, it was 50 feet to the ground. Fortunately, there was a pile of soft garbage below the window. The governors were not seriously injured, but the insult to the Emperor was so great that he sent two armies to Bohemia to bring the defenestrators to justice. Thus began the Thirty Year's War, which took some 30 million casualties during its course.

We denizens of the twentieth century can take some pride in the knowledge that our wars have all been started by more serious considerations than the propulsion of government officials through windows. Every one of these twentieth century wars was initiated by a premeditated military attack:

War	Entering Party	Initiating Event
World War II	France/Britain	German invasion of Poland
World War II	Soviet Union	German invasion of USSR
World War II	United States	Japanese attack at Pearl Harbor
Korean War	United States	North Korean invasion of South Korea
1962 Sino-Indian War	India	Chinese attack
1967 Arab-Israeli War	Egypt	Israeli attack
1973 Arab-Israeli War	Israel	Egyptian and Syrian attack

Of course, one might just as easily conclude from this that we are more Machiavellian in our use of military force than our predecessors and see less need for diplomatic niceties such as initiating crises. Instead, we get right down to the heart of the matter and start fighting immediately.

REACTIONS TO THE INITIATING EVENT

An initiating event is only the first step in the development of a crisis; the next step is the process that each actor in the crisis goes through to determine its reaction to the initiating event. Just about everything that one superpower does is of interest and concern to the other superpower, but always in different degrees. Most of the time, the actions taken by one superpower are not of great interest to the other. Problems arise only when one superpower performs some action that the other deems to be of great concern to itself. Then the first problem facing both superpowers is the precise evaluation of its own interest in the affair.

Many factors are involved in assessing one superpower's interest in another's action. The primary consideration is always the impact of the action on the superpower's security, but this is in itself an involved determination. If the matter is a direct military challenge, then there is little problem ascertaining the danger. For example, the United States had no problem whatever deciding that the installation of intermediate-range ballistic missiles in Cuba in the fall of 1961 constituted a threat to its security. Most provocations are not so simple.

The first consideration is the degree of diplomatic affinity that the superpower feels for the object nation. Thus, the U.S. government was displeased with the Vietnamese invasion of Communist Kampuchea (Cambodia) in the late 1970s, but it had so little concern for Kampuchea that its net interest in the invasion was minimal. On the other hand, should the North Koreans again attack South Korea, the United States would have no reservations about extending full support to this regime with which it maintains close ties.

Related to this is the degree of formal commitment that the superpower has made to the minor country in question. It is essential to honor one's treaty obligations if other treaty promises are to have any meaning. Superpowers that abandon their allies lose prestige.

The next consideration is called *sphere of influence.* The term has a checkered history. During the heyday of European colonialism, it was used as a euphemism for the carving up of the world among the European powers. Even well into the twentieth century, we find it heavily used. For example, the discussions among the Allies toward the close of World War II included many uses of the phrase, with the Soviet Union being given a sphere of influence in Eastern Europe. The idea behind a sphere of influence is that the other powers will not interfere with the activities of the holding power within its own sphere of influence. It is generally recognized that there are constraints on the behavior of the dominant power within its sphere of influence. It cannot, for example, simply annex all territory within its sphere. These constraints, however, are never spelled out. An aggressive power like the Soviet Union can use its sphere of influence assertively, as the Soviet Union has done several times in Eastern Europe by using military force in East Germany, Poland, Hungary, and Czechoslovakia. A superpower can also operate benignly in its sphere of influence, as the United States has done in West Germany.

Nowadays, the meaning of a sphere of influence has been watered down. Minor countries are able to assert their sovereignty more forcefully than in times past. The concept is still useful, but carries less weight than it once did. For example, the United States has a sphere of influence over Latin America. This no longer means that the USA can, for example, invade Nicaragua at will, but it does mean that the Soviet Union had better respect American interests in the region. Similarly, the Soviet Union has a sphere of interest in Eastern Europe, which it exercises aggressively, yet it hesitated to invade Poland in 1981 when the Polish communist regime appeared to be losing control of events. Even though the Soviet Union had invaded Eastern European nations four times previously, it felt qualms about repeating its pattern in the face of strong world opinion that no longer tolerates the most brutal exercises of power.

The third consideration is the actual impact of the provocative action. If the provocation is insignificant in its effect, then there is little need for action, but if it threatens a major change in the world order, then the superpower has little choice but to respond.

The superpower must also consider the importance of the minor country over which the provocation occurs. An American invasion of Grenada, for example, will cause less concern to Soviet planners than an American invasion of East Germany. In the grand geopolitical order, Grenada is about as close to insignificance as a country can get.

Then there is the matter of the superpower's own willingness to engage in assertive diplomatic behavior. "In war," Napoleon said, "the moral is to the physical as three is to one." A superpower's willingness to wield its power can be more important in the world arena than the amount of power itself. Thus Adolf Hitler was able to flout the Treaty of Versailles and annex both Austria and Czechoslovakia because he wielded the small amount of power he actually possessed with determination and ruthlessness. The United States under President Carter was hesitant and unwilling to behave forcefully; it responded to the Soviet invasion of Afghanistan and the Iranian seizure of American hostages with uncertainty. Yet the same nation under President Reagan has demonstrated an aggressiveness and a willingness to rely on military options that frightens much of the world.

These are some of the many considerations that a superpower's leaders will weigh while contemplating their actions during a crisis. As you can see, it is a long list of considerations, making the decision-making process a difficult one.

SUPERPOWER ACTIONS IN CRISES

A superpower always has a large array of options to choose from during a crisis. There are always two extremes: do nothing and declare war. These two extremes are, however, the worst possible choices for a diplomat. Doing nothing constitutes acquiescence to the provocation and encourages further provocations. Declaring war unleashes a catastrophe.

Thus, diplomats and leaders have always sought intermediate solutions, strategies that fall between the two extremes. Sad to say, there are scant few such solutions. When they are found, they can save the world. The American solution to the Soviet closure of land routes to West Berlin in 1948 was the Berlin airlift. This essentially technological solution to a serious diplomatic crisis averted a war. John Kennedy's solution to the problem of the Cuban missiles was the establishment of a naval blockade of Cuba. Ironically, the American solution to the latter problem was analogous to the Soviet action that precipitated the former crisis.

Solutions of this nature tend to be opportunistic. The statesman grabs for whatever he can get. In general, no statesman can count on the appearance of such a stroke of good opportunity to deliver him from a tough crisis. There is only one generalized scheme that can be applied to all modern crises: *brinksmanship*. This is a new word applied to a new concept arising from the impact of the atomic bomb on strategic thinking.

The strategy behind brinksmanship is based on the realization that *neither* side is truly willing to go to nuclear war. If our side can then convince their side that we are seriously contemplating the possibility of launching World War III, then their side will fully realize the gravity of the situation and will back down from the precipice. So goes the logic.

The problem with brinksmanship lies in the execution. Exactly how does one go about convincing the other side that one is preparing for war? Words are the stuff of diplomacy, but no statesman is fool enough to surrender his country's interests on the basis of what might well be a wordy bluff. The statesman needs something more tangible, something that undeniably conveys menacing import to the other side.

Mankind's most awesome and terrifying achievement, the nuclear bomb, has forced us to turn to the simple wisdom of Nature's approach to conflict resolution. The scheme that statesmen have hit upon is the nuclear era's equivalent of a threatened animal's baring its teeth. That simple act simultaneously communicates the creature's ability to inflict damage as well as its willingness to do so. Instead of fangs, we use missiles. Like many animals, we have a well-defined sequence of threatening displays that can be used to communicate willingness to fight. Unlike the display-sequences of most species, ours has yet to achieve the status of a safely unambiguous ritual.

The first step in the sequence is the private diplomatic note. This non-public message is meant to allow the antagonists to resolve their differences without the complications of an audience of clients. If this fails, then the next level of confrontation is the arena of public diplomacy. This can take the form of public denunciations, or escalate to the more serious level of a confrontation in the United Nations. Although such confrontations spark heated debates and grab a great deal of press attention, their significance is frequently overstated. Any crisis that goes no further than the level of the United Nations was never very hot to start with.

The first point at which the superpowers demonstrate deadly seriousness comes when they put their military forces on alert. This telegraphs intent to fight. The armed forces of the United States use a system of *Defense Conditions* (called *DefCon* for short) that specifies their level of preparedness at any given time. There are five levels:

Defense Condition 5: lowest level of preparedness (peace)
Defense Condition 4: low-level alert
Defense Condition 3: highest level of readiness without expectation of imminent combat
Defense Condition 2: attack is considered to be imminent
Defense Condition 1: war

Although this system is used as a means of controlling the armed forces, it can also be used to communicate seriousness of intent to the Soviets. Soviet intelligence is acute enough to quickly detect and report the DefCon level to Moscow, so the American President need not rely solely on words. Simply moving the armed forces to a higher DefCon level will communicate a message to Moscow quickly.

One problem with this approach is that it is vulnerable to counter-brinksmanship. Thus, if we go to DefCon 4, what is to prevent the Soviets from countering by going to their equivalent of DefCon 3? If we can try to intimidate them, why can't they try to intimidate us? And where does it stop? One would hope that the sequence of escalatory sabre-rattling would stop before DefCon 1, but there is another crucial factor to consider: the possibility of things getting out of hand.

One of the great problems of all statesmen is the difficulty they have controlling their own armed forces. From the statesman's point of view, the problem is simple: The armed forces exist to allow the state to enforce its policies in the pursuit of geopolitical advantage. The precise manner in which this tool is used is the sole prerogative of the statesman.

Unfortunately, most military men see the matter differently. In theory, they concede that they are servants of the state; in practice, they compromise their obeisance to state authority with what they call "military necessities." The result is that the outcome of many crises is decided not by diplomatic considerations but by military ones. In effect, the High Command steps forward at the crucial moment in the crisis and declares to civilian authority, "You cannot take that option. For military reasons, you must do this." All too often the result is catastrophic.

For example, in the crucial moment before the onset of World War I, Kaiser Wilhelm lost his nerve and hit upon a wild scheme to reverse the motion of German armies toward war with France and England. At this point Helmuth von Moltke, the Chief of the German General Staff, intervened. Tremendous energies had been expended preparing detailed schedules for troop movements to the front, he argued, and the machinery of mobilization could not be thrown into reverse without destroying it. Mobilization was irreversible; the state would simply have to adapt its policies to the military realities of the armed forces.

A similar problem plagued President Kennedy during the Cuban missile crisis. He wanted the Navy to blockade the island, but did not want any hostile actions taken unless absolutely necessary. He faced resistance from the Navy, which wanted to run a standard blockade. A standard blockade presumes a readiness to engage in hostile activities, something Kennedy had no taste for. Considerable friction arose between the Administration and the Navy.

Fortunately, the Soviets were good enough to back down before hostilities between the Administration and the Navy erupted into open warfare on the streets of Washington.

A much greater problem with the use of military alerts arises from the ease with which military forces create incidents. Military men do not think in terms of the intricacies of diplomatic maneuvers; they operate under a simpler law of the jungle. They tend to use their weapons more readily than diplomats would prefer, often creating incidents which lead to wars. From "the shot heard round the world" at Concord to the killings at Kent State, the tendency for troops in tense situations to create incidents has been demonstrated over and over.

Every statesman lives in dread fear of such incidents. In the critical hours before war was declared in August, 1914, the French government was particularly concerned over just such an incident. It issued an order reading: "By order of the President of the Republic, no unit of the army, no patrol, no reconnaissance, no scout, no detail of any kind, shall go east of the line laid down. Anyone guilty of transgressing will be liable to court-martial."

In the nuclear age, the problems are far greater. In August, 1914, the danger was that some inexperienced junior officer might lose his nerve and shoot at somebody else, inflaming an already sensitive situation. In the nuclear age, an inexperienced junior officer might just have his finger on the button of a nuclear weapon.

MISCALCULATION

The greatest danger in the course of any crisis, after the possibility of a war being started by accident, is the possibility of a miscalculation on the part of the leaders of the nations involved. In fact, miscalculation is the rule, not the exception. Statesmen just don't seem to get all their thinking straight, even when they are making decisions of immense—and possibly irrevocable—import.

On September 1, 1939, Nazi Germany invaded Poland. Both Britain and France, fed up with Hitler's continuing aggression against his neighbors, had promised that they would declare war if Hitler invaded Poland. Hitler did not believe their threats. He went ahead with the invasion. On September 3, 1939, Britain declared war. Hitler was meeting with his foreign minister, Von Ribbentrop, at the time; when he was informed of the British action, he turned to Von Ribbentrop quite agitated and asked savagely, "What now?" Evidently he had started World War II without considering the possibility that Britain might declare war. Oops.

Twenty-five years earlier Kaiser Wilhelm had made a similar blunder. After egging on the Austrians in their confrontation with Serbia, he suddenly found himself face-to-face with a British ultimatum. Later he was to complain, "If only someone had told me beforehand that England would take up arms against us!" Oops.

Statesmen are fallible. The very existence of wars is proof of statesmen's inability to correctly estimate the likely consequences of their actions. How else could two nations submit their dispute to the decision of arms when only one could possibly obtain a favorable decision (and normally, neither does)?

RESOLUTION AND CONSEQUENCES

A crisis can end in one of two ways: One side backs down and accepts some sort of deal, or both sides blunder into a war. The side that backs down always suffers a serious foreign policy setback. In the first place, it loses the issue over which the crisis was triggered. More important, it loses credibility with its opponent. The amount of loss increases with the severity of the crisis. Anybody who takes matters to the brink and then backs down cannot be taken as seriously again.

The loss extends to the other nations of the world. Whenever a nation backs down in a crisis, the other nations note its lack of willpower.

CRISES IN BALANCE OF POWER

Crises in *Balance of Power* are handled in a considerably simplified process. The primary difference between game crises and real-world crises is that the game does not permit creative initiatives such as the American blockade of Cuba during the 1961 Cuban missile crisis. The player is allowed only the possibility of intimidating his opponent through the use of diplomatic threats or military alerts.

The process begins when the player initiates a crisis by questioning an action of his opponent. In the context of this discussion, an action is any operation carried out through the *Policies* menu of the game: troop intervention, weapons shipment, destabilization, economic aid, treaty signature, or application of diplomatic pressure. This action triggers a process of evaluation by the computer opponent. The critical question the computer must decide is, "Should I stand firm and escalate or should I back down?" The following section explains how the answer to the question is computed.

We begin by defining special terms:

Object is the minor country on whom the superpower has acted.

DipAff is the diplomatic affinity of the superpower for *Object*, ranging from −127 to +127. A positive value indicates a warm relationship, a negative value denotes unfriendliness.

DontMess is the measure of the superpower's sphere of influence over *Object*. A high value of *DontMess* means that *Object* is very much within the superpower's sphere of influence, hence, "Don't Mess with dat country!" *DontMess* is normalized to fall between 1 and 15. It is always increased by 8 if an intervention is at stake. Interventions are intrinsically serious business, and a superpower can get pretty self-righteous about the other superpower putting troops anywhere in the world.

Adventurousness is the extent to which a superpower has a demonstrated record of adventurous behavior. Each of the superpowers has its own value of *Adventurousness*, and this value is increased every time the superpower does something bold, and decreased every time the superpower backs down in a crisis. *Adventuróusness* runs from 1 to 127.

Prestige Value is the relative importance of *Object* in the geopolitical order. West Germany has a high prestige value of 200. Nicaragua, with 2, is peanuts.

Obligation springs from any treaty between the superpower and *Object*. A nuclear defense treaty creates an *Obligation* of 127; no treaty creates an *Obligation* of 0.

Hurt is the most difficult concept to explain, and the one over which I expended more effort than any other single element of the game. Simply put, *Hurt* is the amount of damage done to *Object* by the superpower's action. This is a number between −127 and +127. A negative value indicates that the action helped *Object*; a positive

145

value indicates that the action hurt *Object*. In other words, the effect of negative *Hurt* is "help."

Hurt's value is calculated by a variety of special-case formulae. Three general rules govern the amount of *Hurt* created by an action. First, the greater the magnitude of the action, the greater the *Hurt*. More troops intervening or greater diplomatic pressure creates more *Hurt* than less of the same. Second, the amount of *Hurt* depends on the vulnerability of *Object* to the action. Sending weapons to insurgents in a strong, secure country like Great Britain does not create as much *Hurt* as sending weapons to insurgents in a vulnerable nation like the Philippines. Third, some actions are intrinsically more hurtful than others. In general, intervening for rebels is the most hurtful thing that a superpower can do; a full-scale intervention with 500,000 troops will generate 125 points worth of *Hurt*. Just below this comes a full-scale intervention for the government which, depending on the state of the insurgency, could create up to -127 points of *Hurt* but seldom reaches this extreme. Next comes destabilization, the highest level of which will generate 80 points worth of *Hurt*. Economic aid and weapons shipments to the insurgents both generate about 60 points of *Hurt* at their highest levels, but the impact of economic aid is dependent on the state of *Object*'s economy. Diplomatic pressure, weapons shipments to the government, and treaty signatures are all in the lowest level of *Hurt*—at their very strongest levels, they generate values of about ± 40 points of *Hurt*, but again, the conditions in *Object* can modify this.

Remember that positive *Hurt* is real hurt, while negative *Hurt* is actually help. It's a simple idea expressed in oddly mathematical terms.

The meaning of *Hurt* is inverted if the other super-power is helping a friend. For example, if the Soviet Union were to sign a mutual defense treaty with our good friend Canada, the United States would not feel any altruistic pleasure over this friendly move. Instead, it would perceive it as an attempt to compromise its ally and would feel threatened. In other words, a superpower resents not only an attempt to hurt its allies, but also any attempt to help them.

With these terms defined, we are ready for the grand computation:

$$\text{Outrage} = \frac{\text{Hurt} * (\text{Obligation} + \text{DipAff}) * \text{DontMess} * \text{Adventurousness} * \text{Prestige Value}}{128}$$

Outrage is the extent to which the superpower is outraged by the action in question. If the value is negative, then the superpower is pleased.

This equation has a special property that might not be obvious to those who do not handle mathematics regularly. It automatically inverts the meaning of outrage with the circumstances. For example, suppose that the USA hurts a friend of the USSR by attempting to destabilize it. Then *Hurt* will be positive, as will *DipAff* (because the USSR likes *Object*). Since all the other numbers in the formula are positive, the formula has us multiplying lots of positive numbers, and a positive number will thereby obtain. However, suppose that the USA hurts an enemy of the USSR. *Hurt* will still be positive, but now *DipAff* will be negative, because the USSR doesn't like *Object*. Presumably *Obligation* will be 0—why would the USSR sign a treaty with an enemy? Thus, there will be one negative number in the equation, and *Outrage* will therefore be negative: The USSR will be pleased.

Now suppose that the USA does something nice for an enemy of the USSR. *Hurt* will be negative, and so will *DipAff.* Thus we have two negative numbers being multiplied together. This will produce a positive result. Thus, the USSR will experience positive *Outrage* over the action—it will be unhappy about it. In this way, the formula handles a wide variety of situations.

This little equation expresses a lot of ideas about superpower behavior. There are six different terms that go into this equation, and some of them, such as *Hurt,* represent involved computations in their own right. It is easy to admit that all of these ideas belong in the equation; the real test is the relative weighting of the different terms, which is provided in their scaling. For example, *DontMess* is constrained to fall between 1 and 15, while *Prestige Value* can be anything from 1 to nearly 2,000. This means that *Prestige Value* is weighted more heavily than *DontMess.* The other four terms are all constrained to a maximum absolute value of 127, so their weight is intermediate.

This basic computation of *Outrage* is done twice, once for each superpower, regardless of which superpower the computer is playing. In effect, the computer calculates its own *Outrage* over the action and also the human's likely *Outrage* over the action. It then simply adds the two together to obtain the *Outrage Excess.* This is the extent to which its own *Outrage* over the action exceeds the human player's pleasure over the action. Or, if the action pleases the computer, then the *Outrage Excess* is the extent to which the computer's pleasure exceeds the human's *Outrage.*

This can have a strange but justifiable effect when we consider the abnormal situation represented by a country like Iran, which has unfriendly diplomatic relations with *both* superpowers. Any attempt by either superpower to hurt Iran will necessarily create a favorable response from the other superpower, because *DipAff* will always be negative.

Why, the reader might wonder, does the computer attempt to calculate the human's reaction to a policy? Here we get into one of the fundamental notions of game design, and one of the sources of *Balance of Power*'s success as a game: anticipation.

The main difference between a game and most other forms of communication is in the interaction that the game provides. A book, movie, or symphony simply presents its message to its audience, but a game allows the audience to shoot back. The player can try out his own ideas and see how the game responds. Interaction is the source of the appeal of the game. And interaction reaches its highest form when it relies on anticipation. If the computer can guess what the player might do or think, then the computer can respond to that and provide a more interesting interaction with the player.

There is another reason to have anticipation here: realism. A great deal of the energy of the participants in a crisis is expended on trying to figure out how the other side will react to their actions. What are they thinking? What are their motivations? What will they do next? These are the most important questions in the mind of a statesman caught in a crisis.

Thus the use of anticipation in *Balance of Power*. The computer attempts to anticipate the player's likely response to a situation, and adjusts its own behavior accordingly. If it determines that the *Outrage Excess* is positive, then it concludes that it is more justified in pressing its case in the crisis than the human is, so it stands firm. If its *Outrage Excess* is negative, then it concludes that the human feels more strongly about the situation than it does, and it backs down.

Actually, it does mask its true computation during the early stages of a crisis. It adjusts *Outrage Excess* to take into account the seriousness of the crisis:

New Outrage Excess = Outrage Excess + (4 * Crisis Level) + Abs(Random div 1024) − 36

Crisis Level is just a numerical scheme for measuring the level of the crisis. It parallels the DefCon numbering system, but where DefCon stops at 5, *CrisisLevel* continues all the way down to 9. Thus, *CrisisLevel* takes a value of 1 for DefCon 1, 2 for DefCon 2, and so on down to 9 for the lowest level of a crisis. This means that, in the early stages of a crisis, the computer adds something to its *Outrage Excess*. It acts more self-righteous than it knows it has a right to act. In short, it bluffs. But as the crisis gets worse, this term becomes smaller and it acts more on the basis of its serious computations.

The random term is provided to inject a small amount of uncertainty into the process. This value will be, on average, about 16. This will also tend to make the computer seem more belligerent.

The final subtractive term is meant to cancel out some of the belligerence created by the previous two terms. Without it, the computer would always stand absolutely firm on any issue in which it was in the right, and would only back down when it was plainly wrong. By subtracting 36 from the *Outrage Excess*, we make it possible for the player to occasionally bluff the computer successfully.

There is one artifact of this decision-making process that mystifies many players. Suppose that a crisis erupts over some truly insignificant action, such as economic aid to Nigeria. Players often find to their dismay that the computer will escalate right up to DefCon 1 in such situations. Why, they complain, would the computer destroy the world over such a trivial issue?

The answer is, because *you* would destroy the world over such an issue. The computer analyzes the conflict and finds that its *Outrage* over the issue is small, such as 22. It finds, however, that the human pleasure over the issue is even less, such as − 18. When it adds the two numbers together, it gets a + 4 result and concludes that it is justified in taking a firm stand. If the human can ask, "Why would you destroy the world over a measly 22-point crisis?" the computer is even more justified in asking, "Why would you escalate to DefCon 2 over something that was worth only 18 points to you?" It takes two to make a fight.

There are several effects of standing firm and escalating a crisis. First, it worsens relations between the superpowers. This is important for the computation of accidental nuclear war. When tensions are low, accidental nuclear war is unlikely even at DefCon 2. But a high level of tensions makes accidental nuclear war much more likely.

A superpower's integrity is also improved when it stands firm in a crisis, if by doing so it supports a client country. Of course, if it later backs down, everything that it gains is lost. Recall from Chapter 4 that integrity is the measure of a superpower's trustworthiness, and determines the degree to which its treaties are meaningful to its clients.

Finally, the "nastiness" level of the game increases slightly every time a superpower stands firm. *Nastiness* is a background variable that indirectly affects a variety of actions throughout the game.

The higher the *Nastiness*, the greater the chance that the computer will embark on bold, dangerous actions, start crises, and obstinately refuse to back down in crises.

When a superpower backs down, it suffers a number of penalties. The first and most obvious is the loss of prestige, which is calculated from its *Outrage* factor. If you back down when your *Outrage* is very high, you suffer a big loss of prestige.

The loser of a crisis also suffers a degradation of his sphere of influence value *DontMess* for the *Object* of the crisis. If you don't stand up for your sphere of influence, you lose it. Finally, the loser also suffers diminished *Pugnacity*, which will make him seem less threatening to the other superpower. This will encourage further aggressiveness from the other superpower.

How accurate is all this? Not very. Crises are the most individualistic expression of statesmanship. They seldom conform to the generalizations of a computer program. The crisis of August, 1914, bears the unmistakable bluster of Kaiser Wilhelm; the crisis of August, 1939, is the child of Adolf Hitler's deceitful style; the Cuban missile crisis will always be remembered for the brilliant combination of determination and restraint that the Kennedy brothers applied.

The generalized system used in *Balance of Power* to create crises does not reproduce the individualistic style of real-world crises. There is an assembly-line blandness to these artificial crises, a lack of texture and feel that robs them of authenticity. It is true that *all* of the components of the game, from insurgency to coups to interventions, are generalized, but the problem is not so crippling in the other areas of the game. "If you've seen one insurgency, you've seen 'em all" overstates the case, but there is a fundamental similarity to insurgencies that does not exist with crises. Generalizations work fairly well with insurgencies, but poorly with crises.

Nevertheless, the handling of crises in *Balance of Power* covers a great deal of intellectual territory. The complexity of the equation for *Outrage* and the intricacy of the computation of *Hurt* are indicative of the lengths to which I went to capture the nature of modern brinksmanship in a computer program. I can stand by the magnitude of the achievement even while acknowledging its many limitations.

CRISIS: AUGUST, 1914

The first great crisis of the twentieth century was the crisis leading up to the start of World War I. This crisis was completely mismanaged by just about all concerned. The crisis began on June 28, 1914, when the Archduke Ferdinand of Austria-Hungary was assassinated by Serbian extremists in Sarajevo. Austria seized on the crime as a pretext to destroy and absorb Serbia. This was the first Big Mistake of the crisis: Austrian belief that it could take advantage of the tragedy for territorial aggrandizement.

Imperial Germany quickly got into the grand march of mistakes by assuring Austria that, should her actions against Serbia incite a Russian declaration of war, then Germany would declare war on Russia. This assurance violated a fundamental rule of diplomacy: A major power should never give a blank check to one of its client states. The client, emboldened by the power of the major state but lacking the inhibitions that responsibility for such power conveys, will surely embark on adventures that the major power itself would quail at.

Thus emboldened, Austria presented an ultimatum to Serbia; the Serb reply was conciliatory, but Austria rejected it and declared war on July 28. At the moment, all we had was a war between Austria-Hungary and Serbia, with the likely outcome being an Austrian victory and annexation of Serbia.

At this point, Russia decided to add its name to the list of fools. It felt a fundamental geopolitical interest in the Balkans and did not wish to see this area annexed by Austria-Hungary. Russia therefore declared war on Austria-Hungary.

Germany had made the war possible by egging on the Austrians and by giving them guarantees against Russian intervention. Now the Kaiser had to live up to his promises. On August 1, Germany declared war on Russia.

So, by August 1, the war included Germany, Austria-Hungary, Russia, and Serbia. France and Great Britain were not yet involved. However, France had concluded an entente with Russia whereby the French undertook to declare war if Germany should attack Russia. Besides, the French had been spoiling to get back at the Germans ever since since the Franco-Prussian War of 1870. Moreover, the Germans had always assumed that, if war came, France would be in the thick of it. The German war plans meticulously spelled out the steps by which France would be attacked. The Germans were putting these plans in motion well before the French declared war.

This is indicative of the momentum of the situation. The basic fact of the matter was that everybody involved *expected* a major war to develop between the European powers. These expectations were based on two driving forces: a series of grievances that we would now regard as petty, and a desire to establish a new geopolitical order. They were *not* checked by any appreciation of the great potential for slaughter of the weapons of modern warfare.

It was this expectation of war that made the crisis insoluble. The expectation became self-fulfilling. Nations rushed to mobilize their armies in an effort to prepare themselves for the possibility of war, but the very act of mobilization telegraphed intent to fight to the other powers. The frantic efforts of mobilization created an atmosphere of martial activity that made futile any serious efforts toward peace. How can one talk peace when millions of men all over Europe are rushing to arms?

The only government that did not allow itself to be stampeded into war was the British government, and through a cruel twist of fate, its very circumspection served to widen the war. The British had little taste for plunging dirctly into a general European war, but when Germany invaded Belgium in violation of that nation's neutrality, Britain felt compelled to enter the war. Even so, the British took their time, waiting until August 3 to declare war. During the critical hours before the formal declaration, the German heavy battlecruiser *Goeben* was able to elude the British navy in the Mediterranean and sail to Turkey. The arrival of the *Goeben* in Istanbul greatly impressed the Turkish government; that and its subsequent exploits while operating out of Istanbul were instrumental in obtaining the entry of Turkey into the war on the side of Germany.

The fundamental mistake of all the Great Powers in the days before the beginning of hostilities was their refusal to engage in serious diplomatic activity. There was nothing at all like the gradual escalatory system of crises used in *Balance of Power.* For all the actors, there was only one step between peace and war: an ultimatum that gave little room for maneuver. The military mobilization that all nations engaged in was dramatically different from the alerts that the modern powers use. These mobilizations were considered to be irreversible. Mobilization could not be used as a signal of serious intent or a threat of possible action; it was instead tantamount to a declaration of war.

Part of the problem was that the statesmen did not appreciate the seriousness of war in the modern age. They were thinking of a short war like the Franco-Prussian War, which cost "only" 180,000 battle deaths, or about .1% of the populations involved. They thought that the war would be short, violent, and decisive. None of them realized that the war they were leaping into would cost over 7 million battle casualties, or about 6% of the engaged populations.

CRISIS: SEPTEMBER, 1939

Twenty-five years after the crisis that started World War I, the nations of Europe found themselves in the middle of another crisis, this one started by Adolf Hitler over his invasion of Poland on September 1, 1939. For three years, Hitler had been pushing the limits of French and British patience. In 1936 he militarized the Rhineland in violation of the Treaty of Versailles. In 1938 he invaded Austria and the Sudetenland of Czechoslovakia. In 1939 he took over the rest of Czechoslovakia. These actions created a fundamental misapprehension in the minds of the major actors waiting in the wings of the world stage.

Hitler felt that the continuing acquiescence of France and Britain to his persistent aggressions would be maintained. He felt that their past behavior was proof of their lack of concern for events in Eastern Europe. He thought that he had created a diplomatic momentum in his favor that would ensure continuing Allied acquiescence.

The reality was exactly the opposite. The British and French had taken the counsel of patience, thinking that each outrage would be the last, and if only they could endure the latest one, peace would be preserved. By the time Hitler invaded Poland, their patience was exhausted. They had no reservations at all about declaring war. Their decision came as a surprise to Hitler. A top Nazi recorded in his diary on the day war was declared, "Today began the war that the Führer promised us would not begin until 1941."

CRISIS: OCTOBER, 1962

The most serious crisis of the nuclear age was the Cuban missile crisis of October, 1962. The root cause of the crisis was the Soviet decision to place nuclear missiles in Cuba. These missiles were discovered by American aerial reconnaissance on October 16.

The discovery of the Soviet missiles caused a great shock within the Administration. The Soviets had repeatedly assured the United States that they would not place offensive missiles in Cuba. Just one month earlier, the Soviet newspaper *Tass* declared:

> *The Government of the Soviet Union authorized* Tass *to state that there is no need for the Soviet Union to shift its weapons for the repulsion of aggression ... to any other country, for instance Cuba.*

Why did the Soviets do it? Did they seriously believe that the United States would idly accept the placement of hostile nuclear weapons so close to its territory? We can never know the thinking of the Soviet planners, but three arguments create a plausible case for the deployment: (1) the existence of American missiles in Turkey created a justification by analogy; (2) the Soviets felt that missiles in Cuba might deter a feared American invasion of Cuba; (3) Khrushchev judged Kennedy to be a weak leader who would back down from the challenge.

On all three points, the Soviets had miscalculated. Kennedy had already ordered the removal of the American missiles from Turkey; there were no plans for an American invasion of Cuba; and Kennedy would not back down. These three miscalculations made the crisis possible.

With the missiles in place and the Americans aware of them, the ball was in Kennedy's court. We have good records of the difficult deliberations of the Administration. Six major types of response were considered: (1) do nothing; (2) diplomatic response; (3) deal with Castro; (4) blockade Cuba; (5) air strike on the missiles; and (6) invade Cuba.

None of the options looked promising. The first two were unlikely to produce results, especially since the missiles would be ready for combat in two weeks. The Soviets could easily stall a diplomatic initiative until the missiles were ready; then the American military options would be all but eliminated. The third approach foundered on the fact that the missiles were operated by Soviet technicians over whom Castro had no control. The last three options were military and offered the greatest chance of success while posing the greatest risk of war.

One of the surprising aspects of the Administration's deliberations was the active role that the military took in the decision-making process. In theory, the military operates under the Clausewitzian doctrine that "war is the extension of policy to other means" and leaves the policy decisions to the politicians, confining itself to advising the policy-makers on the capabilities and limitations of the military forces. In the case of the Cuban missile crisis, the military leaders assumed a far more active role, arguing long and hard for the invasion option.

For a while, the Administration leaned toward the option of the surgical air strike. Their thinking was that they could destroy the missile sites and present the Soviet Union with a fait accompli in the same way that the Soviets had hoped to present the Americans with a fait accompli. But the option foundered on the pig-headedness of the American military leaders, who refused to accept the assignment given them and instead tried to impose their own thinking on the Administration. Instead of planning a surgical air strike that would neatly destroy the missiles, the Air Force wanted a massive air offensive involving the full weight of the Air Force directed against not just the missiles, but also a variety of peripheral support installations. When Administration officials protested that this was more firepower than they wanted, the Air Force stretched the truth and declared that it would not be possible to guarantee the destruction of the missiles without so massive an attack. The option was discarded.

The Administration then fell back on the blockade option. The special attraction of the blockade was that it clearly communicated the Administration's willingness to use force over the problem, yet in itself created no cause for immediate retaliation. Moreover, a blockade was an intrinsically slow-moving policy option that would give the Kremlin plenty of time to consider its response.

Even then, the Administration had serious

problems getting its military to execute its orders. The Navy's attitude was that, once the President had decided on a blockade, the details of the blockade itself were not within the authority of the President to change. When Kennedy ordered a change in the radius of the blockade, his order was resisted; when he pressed, the Navy accepted the order but, without Kennedy's knowledge, failed to carry it out. At another point, Robert McNamara, the Secretary of Defense, confronted Chief of Naval Operations Anderson with detailed questions on exactly how the Navy intended to handle a number of delicate situations. McNamara met angry resistance at this "intrusion" into Navy affairs. The meeting broke up with the Navy man's remark, "Now, Mr. Secretary, if you and your Deputy will go back to your offices, the Navy will run the blockade."

Throughout all of this the President and his advisors were acutely aware of the tremendous risks that they were taking. Kennedy was later to estimate that the chances of nuclear war had been between one in three and one in two. At one point he observed, "The great danger and risk in all of this is a miscalculation—a mistake in judgment" (Allison 1971). He had recently read historian Barbara Tuchman's book *The Guns of August* detailing the events leading up to World War I and was painfully aware of the ease with which statesmen can get themselves into a war.

The blockade went into effect on October 24. It was not, however, an airtight blockade; Kennedy allowed a number of Communist ships to pass through, despite the heated objections of his military advisors. He wanted to give Khrushchev more time to think things over.

At the same time, Kennedy demonstrated his determination to prevail by increasing the military pressure in a number of ways. He mobilized ground forces in the Southern states in an obvious preparation for a possible invasion of Cuba. He stepped up aerial military activity over Cuba. In short, he made it plain that the United States was preparing for a full-scale war over Cuba.

The combination of unambiguous military action and careful restraint had the desired effect. On Wednesday, October 24, the Communist ships en route to Cuba stopped dead in the water, many of them just short of the blockade line. Dean Rusk, the American Secretary of State, made the classic remark on brinksmanship: "We're eyeball to eyeball, and I think the other fellow just blinked."

The crisis was not over; it went through several more dangerous twists and turns before it was resolved. On Friday, October 26, the Administration received a proposal from Khrushchev that appeared to provide the basis for an acceptable resolution to the crisis. On Saturday, as they were considering their response to this proposal, the Soviets broadcast a *second* proposal, far harsher than the first. This put the members of the ExComm (the Executive Committee that Kennedy had selected to handle the crisis) in a quandary. Which proposal should they respond to? The Soviet position was now ambiguous.

The ingenious solution to the quandary was

proposed by Robert Kennedy: ignore the second proposal and respond favorably to the first. The Administration simply behaved as if the second proposal had never been made. And this became the basis for the resolution of the crisis.

THE OCTOBER WAR CRISIS, 1973

On October 6, 1973, Egypt and Syria attacked Israel. After taking heavy casualties and suffering serious reverses, the Israelis regained the initiative and trapped the Egyptian Third Army in the Suez. At this point, the Americans were able to obtain a cease-fire, but a curious sequence of misunderstandings generated a crisis between the United States and the Soviet Union.

Despite its agreement to the cease-fire, Israel was eager to finish off the Egyptian Third Army and continued its attacks. These attacks triggered desperate efforts by Anwar Sadat to enlist aid in enforcing the cease-fire. The Americans pressured the Israelis to stop their attacks. Stalling for time, the Israelis offered to permit American observers located in Tel Aviv to journey to the front and verify Israeli compliance with the cease-fire. Kissinger was not impressed by the Israeli offer but duly reported it to the Egyptians. Then came an amazing turn of events: Sadat "accepted" the American offer to dispatch troops to enforce the cease-fire from the *Egyptian* side. The real offer had been an *Israeli* offer to permit a few American soldiers to *observe* the cease-fire from the *Israeli* side. Whether this was a simple misunderstanding or a deliberate misinterpretation of the original Kissinger note will never be known. Far more important, Sadat announced that he was making the same formal offer to the Soviet Union.

The implications of this offer were profound. If the Soviets complied with the Egyptian request for direct intervention, then Israeli forces would be in direct combat with Soviet troops. The Soviet Union would not send troops to lose a battle; they would send whatever was necessary to defeat Israeli forces. The United States would not be able to stand by and watch its ally defeated. It, too, would intervene, and thus American troops would square off against Soviet troops in the Middle East. It was a frightening prospect, one that had to be prevented.

Events moved quickly. In the hours after Sadat's message, the United States sent a series of messages to the Soviet Union in an attempt to foreclose the more frightening options. Kissinger also worked to insure that events in the United Nations did not add fuel to the crisis. Within a few hours, however, the Soviet Union sent a message to the United States that amounted to an ultimatum. The message said,

> *Let us together, the USSR and the USA, urgently dispatch to Egypt the Soviet and American military contingents, to insure the implementation of the decision of the Security Council [the cease-fire] .... If you find it impossible to act jointly with us in this matter, then we should ... consider the question of taking appropriate steps unilaterally ....*
>
> (Years of Upheaval)

In other words, the Soviets were saying, "We are sending military forces into Egypt, with or without you." The nightmare scenario was unfolding.

Kissinger convened a meeting in the White House. Here began the process of anticipation that plays so strong a role in resolving crises. In Kissinger's words, "The participants weighed Soviet actions, motivations, and intentions" *(Years of Upheaval)*. At 11:41 P.M. on Wednesday, October 24, the armed forces of the United States were put on DefCon 3. In addition, the 82nd Airborne Division was put on notice for possible movement, and various naval units in the area were instructed to move quickly to the eastern Mediterranean.

Meanwhile, the Soviets were making their own military moves. The East German army had been put on alert. Soviet aircraft were making ready to transport troops to Egypt. Diplomatically, the Soviets were menacingly quiet.

At 5:00 A.M. on the morning of Thursday, October 25, the Administration sent a stiff note to Brezhnev warning that unilateral Soviet intervention in the Middle East would be resisted by force. The cards were on the table.

The showdown was defused by Anwar Sadat. By 8:00 A.M. he had sent to the Administration a letter modifying his position in a crucial fashion. Instead of requesting American and Soviet troops, he was now requesting an international force, which by custom excluded troops from the superpowers. At a stroke, the crisis was over. The Soviets, with the rug pulled out from underneath them, backed off.

THE UNINCLUDED FACTORS

The real world of geopolitics is a complicated place. Dozens or even hundreds of factors such as military power, diplomacy, economics, and religion influence geopolitical behavior. In the preceding chapters, I have discussed the four primary processes that *Balance of Power* includes: insurgency, coups, Finlandization, and crises. However, *Balance of Power* is a *game*, not a simulation; I have deliberately chosen to emphasize these four factors at the expense of others. The limited amount of RAM (the computer's memory), the need for clear conflict, and the requirement that the game be easily understood by the player forced me to maintain a brutal editorial discipline with the game. I removed or failed to include a number of processes that rightly deserved a place in a proper simulation of geopolitics.

The process by which I chose some factors for inclusion while rejecting others was not a matter of moving through a checklist and placing check marks in front of some items and Xs in front of others. The factors that went into the game grew naturally from fundamental considerations about my goals in designing the game, and some of those that didn't make it into the game were not rejected, but simply were never considered because they did not flow naturally from these fundamental considerations. Thus, one of the central concepts in the game was the notion of superpower conflict being expressed through conflicts in minor countries. This naturally led to the use of insurgency and the options superpowers have for supporting one side or the other in an insurgency. Conversely, arms control never entered into the design because it is not a channel for superpower conflict but rather a (frequently failed) vehicle for superpower cooperation.

In this chapter I will discuss some of the factors that, for one reason or another, never made it into *Balance of Power:* trade, multipolarity and neutralism, minor-country wars, arms control, human rights, and positive initiatives.

TRADE

Trade between nations is an important element of their relationships for many reasons. First, trade allows nations to specialize their economies more closely to the areas of their greatest strengths and weaknesses, and to take advantage of the economies of scale created by heavy capitalization in other countries. For example, intensive trade links have made it possible for some East Asian nations to break out of their poverty. Their large populations were once seen only as a liability, but by concentrating on heavy utilization of their abundant cheap labor, they have been able to build up their economies rapidly. These same nations enjoy access to manufactured products, such as telecommunications systems, from the developed nations that would require a prohibitively expensive industrial base to develop domestically. Increased trade has also allowed the developed nations to concentrate their energies on making further refinements to their industrial base, without diverting their energies to the acquisition of raw materials or the utilization of great amounts of labor that the underdeveloped nations now supply. Trade confers a second benefit in providing goods or raw materials that may not be available domestically at any reasonable price. Much of the world's supply of many crucial minerals comes from South Africa. Some nations, such as Japan, have very little in the way of natural resources and must import all of their raw materials. Similarly, most of the world's underdeveloped nations have little indigenous manufacturing capacity and must rely on imports from the developed nations for many of their manufactured items, especially those requiring the most advanced manufacturing technologies.

The value of trade has been demonstrated by the fact that it is increasing worldwide. In the last twenty years, total world trade as a percentage of total world Gross Domestic Product has increased markedly. The increase in the absolute value of total world trade is even more dramatic: Total annual world trade in constant dollars increased from $246 billion in 1969 to over $1 trillion in 1978. Apparently, trade confers enough benefits to make it highly desirable to many countries.

Thus, external trade is an important and desirable component of any national economy. This fact has not been lost on diplomats, who have learned to use their ability to selectively grant or deny trade privileges as a diplomatic weapon. Over the years this weapon has been polished and refined, so that there are now a variety of options open to the statesman: trade barriers, restrictions, boycotts, and embargoes.

TRADE BARRIERS

First comes the normal array of trade barriers, quotas, duties, tariffs, and other restrictions on full free trade. These are seldom used as diplomatic weapons. Instead, they are most often expressions of economic policy. Thus, the Japanese restrictions on American products entering its economy are not caused by diplomatic strains, but are instead an expression of economic goals. Some of the American responses to Japanese imports, such as the threatened restrictions on automobile imports which have led to voluntary restraints on shipments of automobiles to the United States by the Japanese automakers, are simply economic in nature, while others, such as the imposition of duties on some Japanese electronic components as a partial response to restrictive Japanese regulations on the sale of American electronic components in Japan, are meant to be diplomatic signals. Such actions, of course, can lead to diplomatic strains between countries.

Trade barriers of various kinds are so common that they have little direct value as diplomatic weapons. Such barriers are commonly erected by a variety of countries for reasons having little to do with diplomacy. It is hard to impress somebody with the seriousness of your intentions by slapping them with restrictions that are business as usual for most of the world. It is the *absence* or *removal* of such trade barriers that is significant diplomatically. The United States designates this condition as *Most Favored Nation* status and extends it only to its best friends.

RESTRICTIONS

Next there is the limited restriction on specific items. Normal trade relations are allowed, but certain goods may not be traded to the subject nation. Such restrictions normally apply only to weapons and strategic materials. For example, the United States restricts the export of weapons systems to unfriendly nations. It also restricts the sale of sensitive equipment that could be used in the manufacture of nuclear weapons to all non-nuclear nations. A policy of this nature does not imply unfriendliness, only wariness.

BOYCOTTS

Next comes the trade boycott. This is a full-scale refusal to allow any form of trade between the two countries. The odd thing about such a boycott is that it hurts both countries equally. That is, if the trade between two countries is mutually profitable, then loss of that trade is a mutual loss. If one of the nations is supplying goods that simply cannot be obtained elsewhere, then the other nation will suffer a greater economic dislocation, but the disparity is mitigated by the fact that such a monopolistic situation would normally mean very high profits for the seller, profits that would be lost in a boycott. The trade boycott is most often practiced by a wealthy nation against a poorer nation. In this case, although both nations suffer equal absolute loss, the proportional loss is larger in the poorer nation.

The trade boycott by a single nation against another nation is seldom effective. The United States placed a trade boycott on Cuba after the accession of Castro. If ever there was an ideal case for a trade boycott, this was it. Cuba was a small, poor country, and the majority of Cuban trade was with the United States. This trade boycott, more than any other, should have been crippling. But it was a failure. Cuba arranged to sell its primary export crop, sugar, to the Eastern bloc nations. There was some economic dislocation associated with the sudden change, but the Cubans prevailed.

Trade boycotts have at best a temporary effect. Within a few years, almost any economy can adjust itself to accommodate the new situation.

EMBARGOES

The most powerful diplomatic weapon is the multination embargo. If a group of nations constituting the bulk of the supply or demand for any given good can agree to collectively embargo another nation or group of nations, they have a powerful diplomatic weapon. The most dramatic demonstration of this was the Arab oil embargo of 1973-74. In the history of international trade, there has never been a more propitious situation for use of a trade embargo as a diplomatic weapon. The price of oil was much lower than its effective market value, most of the production was concentrated in a few nations sharing common political aims, and the oil itself was crucial to the economic well-being of the industrialized nations. Angered by American support of Israel in the

1973 October War, the Arab members of OPEC finally found the unity to take a strong position. In a series of strokes, OPEC cut production of oil, raised prices dramatically, and announced an embargo against the United States and the Netherlands. Together, these actions were effective in cutting the supply of oil to the embargo's victims.

The effect on the United States was profound. The oil shock plunged the nation into a recession, and the steady rise of oil prices inhibited economic growth for the remainder of the decade. Long gasoline lines formed, buyers of gasoline were limited to ten gallons per visit, and the price of fuel-efficient cars shot up. A plan for the national rationing of gasoline was put together and rationing coupons were printed. American society staggered under the impact of the embargo.

But even this, the most effective trade embargo in history, had its shortcomings. The United States refused to modify its Middle East policies under the pressure of the embargo. After a few months, the Administration began to mutter darkly about retaliatory moves, and the American public was openly discussing an invasion of Saudi Arabia. (One producer of board wargames, SPI, later published a game on just such a hypothetical invasion. It was called *Oil War*.) Having achieved a great deal—though not as much as they had hoped for—and starting to feel nervous about the growing American anger, the Arab oil producers called off the embargo. They had scored a limited political victory.

SUMMARY

My point in this long discussion of trade restrictions in international relations is that the trade weapon is not a particularly effective one. Trade barriers normally evoke only retaliatory measures. Boycotts are easily defeated by going to other suppliers or consumers. Even organized embargoes can be broken up by economic adjustment or military sabre rattling.

Paradoxically, this is one source of its value to diplomats. Trade weapons don't do much harm, yet they do have a psychological effect. Use of the trade weapon is akin to the slapping of a gentleman's face with one's glove: It is a symbolic act that inflicts little real damage. It can mollify the volatile masses of citizens who imprudently scream for blood, without irreparably damaging relations between nations.

The other advantage of the trade weapon is its precision and controllability. The greatest fear of the modern statesman is that of losing control of events over some stupid incident. This problem is greatest when troops are involved. When you send large numbers of heavily armed people into a powder keg, your chances of having everything go according to plan are very low. Some rosy-cheeked 19-year-old will misinterpret a shadow in the dark and create an international incident. Trade restrictions are invulnerable to this danger. Moreover, trade restrictions do not invite escalation. In the tit-for-tat world of diplomacy, eliminating trade removes the tat.

Thus, trade weapons in diplomacy are not as powerful as many people would think, but they are safe and reliable, and they seldom make matters any worse. That's why trade weapons will continue to be used by diplomats in the future.

TRADE AND BALANCE OF POWER

Why is trade not included in *Balance of Power*? As it happens, I had included trade in the earliest versions of the game. I had painstakingly researched the trade relations between every pair of nations in my sample, which were some 3,800 pairs in all. I had then typed in the results of my research. Then I tore it all out of the game. Why? First, these trade numbers took up too much RAM. The program was tight on RAM from the very beginning, and the day came when I simply had to make more space. Because the trade numbers consumed a considerable amount of RAM, they were an obvious candidate. I ultimately chose to eliminate trade because it is a less decisive diplomatic weapon than those that I left in the game. It is a second-order tactic requiring considerable subtlety and finesse. *Balance of Power* is an introductory game; I felt it necessary to include the primary factors before moving to the more subtle ones.

*M*ULTIPOLARITY AND NEUTRALISM

Balance of Power presents a bipolar view of the world. The world is divided into two camps, those of the USA and the USSR. All other nations of the world exist solely in relation to this polarization. A nation's foreign policy is measured by its position on a scale between the poles of the two superpowers.

This is an overly simplistic view of the world. There is another way to view the world—the multipolar view. In the multipolar view, the United States and Soviet Union are merely the two most powerful nations in the world. The world is seen as a collection of sovereign states, each with its own policy interests and capabilities. Nations are bound to and repelled by each other through a complex web of affinities and animosities.

The multipolar view is a more complex model of

the world community. It allows a wider range of interactions between states. There are two important concepts in particular that find easy expression in the multipolar view: neutralism, and the emergence of China as a superpower.

Neutralism is the policy stance of those nations that do not wish to be identified with either the Soviet camp or the American one. Austria, Sweden, and Switzerland are neutralist. A good many Third World countries are also purportedly neutral, but they prefer to use the term "nonaligned." In some cases, such as India, this term is appropriate, for India has steered a careful course between the superpowers. In other cases the term is misleading. For example, Cuba has gone to some length to establish its position as the leader of the nonaligned movement, but few nations accept the fiction that Cuba is in practice nonaligned.

The concept of neutralism just doesn't fit into the bipolar view of the world. Staunch supporters of the bipolar view often take the position that every country in the world is either "with us or agin' us." A genuinely neutralist country like India is suspected of diplomatic opportunism—of attempting to play off the superpowers against each other.

Another important concept that multipolarity encourages is the developing role of China as the world's third superpower. For the next few decades, China will remain a minor character on the world stage, but this can change quickly if China can master its economic problems. Its huge and energetic population could quickly make it a major force in the world economic order, and its political stance as a Communist state with fundamental disputes with the Soviet Union make it a natural "third force" in the delicate geopolitical balance.

Again, the bipolar view of the world sees China solely in terms of how pro-Western or how pro-Soviet it is, and so is blind to the much more likely outcomes.

The emergence of China could end the dangerously unstable situation in which the two superpowers find themselves. In a bipolar world, the only check on one superpower is the other. If you can destroy the other superpower, you have no rivals. The situation is drastically different in a tripolar world. To achieve global dominance, one superpower must destroy both of the other superpowers. Assuming that all three superpowers have roughly the same total power, this is quite out of the question. Moreover, the possibility of two superpowers forming a condominium against the third superpower is remote, for each of the conspiring superpowers would know that, once the third superpower was eliminated, they would be back to the bipolar world of today, with no guarantees of security. The weaker superpower would never go along with so suicidal a plan. A tripolar world would see lots of diplomatic maneuvering, many shifting pairings between superpowers, but it would be fundamentally stable.

MULTIPOLARITY AND BALANCE OF POWER

If multipolarity is so superior to bipolarity as an explanation of the world geopolitical order, why then does *Balance of Power* use a bipolar view? For three reasons: first, bipolarity is simpler and easier to understand; second, bipolarity is more intrinsically conflict-oriented than multipolarity, and games demand conflict; and third, bipolarity is not such a bad description of the world of the 1980s.

As with trade, early versions of *Balance of Power* did include multipolarity. But just as trade ran up against the memory

181

limitations of the Macintosh, so did multipolarity. For example, one of the most important concepts in the game is a quantity that I call "diplomatic affinity," which is the degree to which two countries "like" each other. In early versions of *Balance of Power,* diplomatic affinity was a two-dimensional array with 62 columns by 62 rows, although the matrix was collapsed along its diagonal to save space. This still consumed some 3800 bytes of space. It was necessary to have such a large array because multipolarity required that I record the diplomatic affinity of each of the 62 countries of the world for every other country: 62 countries times 62 countries. Later on, I reluctantly chose to eliminate multipolarity, and the diplomatic affinity array was changed dramatically. It became a much shorter two-dimensional array with only two rows and 62 columns—one row for each of the two superpowers, because it was only necessary to record how each country felt about each of the two superpowers.

Players of *Balance of Power* should realize that bipolarity is not held in high esteem in most countries of the world. Indeed, one source of friction between the United States and its allies is the American fixation on a bipolar view of the world. "Americans," our allies complain, "always see the world in terms of *us* versus *them.* The real world is more complex than that." For example, we tend to view the populist Sandinista revolution in Nicaragua solely as a manifestation of communist expansion in the Western Hemisphere, while most other countries view Nicaragua in far less sinister terms. They see a populist revolution that overthrew a brutal dictator. Overactive American imaginations, in the eyes of many foreigners, see the Dark Hand of Moscow in every local fracas.

So which is right—bipolarity or multipolarity? There is no clear answer. These two concepts are not answers to questions, but rather ways of looking at problems. Each of the two views helps illuminate the complex events of the world scene. *Balance of Power* only shows the bipolar view. Players should be aware of the multipolar view, for it explains some aspects of international behavior not addressed by the bipolar view.

Minor country wars

Another factor that was removed from early versions of *Balance of Power* was the ability of minor countries to declare war on each other. Such wars between minor countries have been a significant contributor to superpower tensions, and have on many occasions been the precipitating factor in major wars. World War I was ignited over a sideshow war between Austria-Hungary and Serbia. The major powers had no direct wish for a war but were dragged in by their commitments to their minor-country allies. An even more clear-cut case was the Korean War. Here were two very minor countries, North Korea and South Korea, each with its own protector, China and the United States. Neither the United States nor China had any desire to fight a war in 1950. But when North Korea invaded South Korea, the United States felt compelled to defend its junior partner. Later, when the United States invaded North Korea, China felt compelled to defend *its* ally. Thus, two unwilling giants were dragged into a confrontation they had no desire to pursue solely because of the actions of their allies.

This is a major flaw in the nation-state system. It arises from the conflict between the notion of sovereignty and mutual defense obligations. Sovereignty is the notion that a nation-state is absolutely free to pursue its own interests, with no externally imposed restrictions on its behavior. Sovereignty is to a nation as freedom is to an individual. However, the sovereignty of states is compromised by their treaty obligations. A case in point is the relationship between China and North Korea. Now, in theory, a mutual defense treaty is written to guarantee assistance to a nation *only* if it is attacked. In other words, China was under no formal obligation to assist North Korea, because North Korea had initiated the war. In practice, however, things work out differently. Powerful nations provide their client states with mutual defense treaties for sound reasons. For sound strategic reasons, it was in China's best interest for North Korea to survive, regardless of whether North Korea had started the war. Consequently, China had no choice but to intervene.

So here is the dilemma: Where does sovereignty end and client status begin? If North Korea had been a truly sovereign nation, it would have suffered the consequences of its mistake and been conquered. If, on the other hand, it was a proper Chinese client, then it would not have acted without Chinese direction, and the invasion would have been unlikely. The unfortunate fact is that North Korea was sovereign enough to start the war and client enough to get Chinese support when it started to lose. That is a dangerous combination.

Lest the reader think that this was a Communist mistake that we would never repeat, I shall bring up the subject of the American relationship with Israel. Israel is a sovereign state, and has demonstrated its sovereignty time and time again with its wars with Arab states. The United States cannot dictate policy to the Israeli government, yet is compelled by precedent and treaty relationships to stand by it. Once before, in 1973, we went toe-to-toe with the Soviet Union in support of Israel. We have no assurances that our relationship with Israel in another Arab-Israeli war will not bring us into another confrontation with the Soviets, one that we might not survive.

Arms control

Another factor not included in *Balance of Power* is arms control—the attempt by the superpowers to limit the growth of their arsenals. Arms control is commonly held to be one of the most important theaters of superpower interaction; its absence in *Balance of Power* surprises some players. Why was it not included?

The most important reason for my excluding arms control in the game is the complexity of the matter. Arms control is one of those endlessly intricate issues on which one could spend many years of study. Moreover, the fundamentals of the field keep changing with new technologies. In the late 1960s the issue was anti-ballistic missile defenses; in the 1970s the MIRV (multiple independent re-entry vehicle) became the major issue that destabilized the arms race; now, in the 1980s, the issue is President Reagan's Strategic Defense Initiative, popularly known as Star Wars.

Any attempt to include arms control in *Balance of Power* would strangle over the dilemma posed by the complexity of the issue. If arms control were presented in a simple fashion appropriate to the needs of the game, it would be trivialized. If it were presented with any reasonable degree of thoroughness, it would dominate the game. In my judgment as a game designer, arms control cannot fit into a game on geopolitics. Perhaps it would be possible to design a game devoted to arms control, and indeed I have worked on just such a game (discussed in Chapter 8), without success. But it *is* another game.

The reader might ask, "Why did you do a game on geopolitics instead of a game on arms control?" Here we enter the realm of my own personal taste. I can present my own opinions here, but I cannot offer them as anything more than the opinions of one citizen, and not even an expert one at that. I do not share the common opinion that the most efficacious way to save the human race from nuclear war is to eliminate nuclear weapons. This opinion requires some explanation.

How are we to prevent a nuclear war? There are two fundamental strategies: prevent a superpower war and prevent nuclear weapons. The first strategy does allow for the continued existence of nuclear weapons but attempts to avoid their use. The second strategy admits the possibility of a superpower war but attempts to guarantee that such a war be non-nuclear.

I believe that the second strategy is not the one most likely to achieve success. In the first place, the central concept of arms control is crippled by a fundamental dilemma. The premise is that a nation can agree to a treaty that requires it to abandon its only means of enforcing the treaty. Any treaty eliminating nuclear weapons entirely creates the unacceptable situation for each side that, should the other side cheat, the honest side would be helpless to resist the demands of the cheater, much less enforce its own demands for compliance. Despite all the work on "national technical means of verification," the "bomb in the basement" remains the great bugaboo of arms control.

Our historical experience only lends credence to the theoretical impasse. From their earliest days, nuclear weapons have evoked calls for their elimination. Everybody wants them reduced or eliminated, yet their numbers have grown with each passing year. The diplomats negotiate endlessly and the best we have accomplished is a temporary slackening of the pace of growth. After twenty-five years of serious effort, the total number of warheads has grown from about 100 to about 50,000—a growth rate of 28% per year. Arms control remains a field with high hopes and few results.

On the other hand, I do think that it is possible for the superpowers to learn how to restrain their global competition in such a way as to prevent the possibility of a nuclear war. There is historical evidence to support this. Despite the fluctuations of super-power relations, there has been a slow backing away from the precipice of nuclear war. Our relations with the Soviet Union may not be warmer today than they were, say, thirty years ago, but the two nations do have a clearer understanding of the limits of each other's patience. The Soviets may grumble about our attack on Libya, and we may grouse about their invasion of Afghanistan, but we have come a long way from the Cuban missile crisis, when we tottered on the very brink of nuclear war. For all of the heated rhetoric, both sides are more careful about upsetting the other on fundamental issues. In short, over the last forty years of the USA-USSR competition, we have slowly and painfully hammered out a clumsy *modus vivendi.*

I do not present diplomacy as the ideal solution to the problem of nuclear war, for even diplomacy fails. But it is our best bet, I think. And that is a fundamental assumption behind *Balance of Power.* The game is about geopolitics, not arms control, because I believe that therein lies the surest path to successful avoidance of nuclear war. I do not expect the reader to accept my opinions as compelling, for the matter is too complex to admit anything like certainty, especially in a discussion only a few paragraphs long. I only explain my decision to design a game on geopolitics instead of the arms race. (Confusingly enough, I originally chose to call the game *Arms Race*, even though I knew it wasn't about arms races; I just couldn't think of a catchy title about geopolitics.)

HUMAN RIGHTS AND OTHER FACTORS

Some players have objected to the air of ruthless competition incorporated in the game. The scoring system requires the player to hurt unfriendly governments and support friendly ones, regardless of their moral worth. Some have pointed out that this approach introduces a subtle bias towards confrontation into the game, and observe that there are a variety of other geopolitical goals of an American government. The one most often mentioned is human rights. Why were no considerations of human rights included in the game?

As it happens, the game did once have a more complex scoring system that included far more than just human rights. There were a number of factors for measuring success, including human rights, war-related deaths, prestige, and total world economic growth. The intent of all these separate scores was to make it possible for players to bring their own values to the game. A liberal could play the game for a good human-rights score, while a conservative might play for economic growth or prestige. I did not want to impose my own values on the player.

The problem was, people *wanted* me to impose my values on them! The early playtesters all complained about the lack of a clear set of goals for the game. They wanted the game to tell them how well they had done. Here we run into one of the expectations arising from the fact that *Balance of Power* is a game. People want to win it according to some defined standard of performance. I tried a compromise. I cut down on the number of dimensions. Not good enough; the playtesters still complained. My editor hammered away on this issue, arguing that the game lacked focus and clearly defined goals. I eventually caved in and eliminated all but the single measure of performance: prestige.

Players should remember that there are many measures of success on the world stage. This problem is ultimately a question of values. What do we want to accomplish in the world? For ages, there was an easy answer to that question: The goal of nations was to attain hegemony over all potential rivals. Only such hegemony guaranteed security. The United States is the first major power in world history to back off from the goal of world domination. Perhaps our wealth makes world domination seem pointless; perhaps our isolationist past makes us shy away from global responsibilities; perhaps our geographical position gives us a feeling of security that makes hegemony seem unnecessary; perhaps we recognize the hopelessness of the task. What, then, should our goals be?

There are many possibilities. We could pursue human rights and the establishment of a just world order. Perhaps we should more energetically attempt to promulgate democracy. Perhaps we should look towards material development and the elimination of hunger. Perhaps we should strive to eliminate the local wars that take thousands of lives every year. *Balance of Power* can provide no answers to these questions.

"POSITIVE INITIATIVES"

One left-wing organization complained that the game lacked "positive initiatives." The complaint was unclear as to the precise meaning of "positive initiatives," but there is a valid objection here: The game does focus on the more negative aspects of geopolitics. The emphases on insurgencies, on military power, and on coups all give the game a pugnacious feel. Where is the possibility for something like Henry Kissinger's shuttle diplomacy, or Jimmy Carter's human-rights initiatives? Why does the game not permit "creative initiatives"?

Here we run into another fundamental limitation imposed by the nature of the game. It would have been desirable to allow the player to engage in such creative initiatives and pursue special strategies. The problem lies in the word *special*. A special strategy requires consideration of special factors, and you can't consider them unless they are included. What "special factors" should be included in a game about geopolitics? The personalities of individual leaders? The internal political makeup of each government? Some cultural or historical factor about which a particular government might be particularly sensitive and defensive?

It is possible to include such special factors in a computer program, but one quickly runs out of RAM space trying to include all of them. Computer programs with many special factors do not operate well. They work best with generalized principles that can be universally applied. Thus, *Balance of Power* treats each nation in a generalized manner, applying algorithms to its behavior in the same fashion that it treats every other nation. For some reason, I know not why, the negative, brute-force techniques do seem more amenable to generalized treatment than do positive initiatives. This may reflect some grand truth of international relations, or it may be a misleading artifact of the application of the computer. In any event, the reader should be aware of the problem.

CONCLUSION

These are some of the factors that were left out of *Balance of Power.* Surely they are not all the unincluded factors; some factors were left out of the game because of my own limited understanding of international relations. Some of them were left out because of the biases that make up my own world view. Some were left out for technical reasons or because of limited memory space. It is easy to lament these shortcomings of the game, to imagine how much more interesting it would be with more features and more processes. I feel no regret over these deficiencies, though. I am pleased with the final balance between completeness and accessibility in the game. Aficionados will plead for more detail while novices beg for simplification. If anything, I erred in the direction of excessive thoroughness.

I cannot and would not present *Balance of Power* as a definitive statement on geopolitics, nor as even an unbiased and evenhanded representation. It is too intensely personal a statement.

STRATEGY FOR BALANCE OF POWER

he purpose of this book is to develop the ideas presented in *Balance of Power* and extend the player's understanding of those concepts. However, some players will also expect that, having understood these concepts better, they should be able to play the game better. This chapter makes explicit suggestions on how to play *Balance of Power* more successfully.

CRISES

Balance of Power is most often lost in a crisis, either by blowing up the world or by caving in. A crisis can easily place several hundred points of prestige at stake; by contrast, replacing the Sandinista government in Nicaragua with a very pro-American regime would be worth less than ten points. Thus, effective crisis management is the central requirement of the game.

Crises are won or lost *before* they begin. That is, the player's preparations for a crisis will determine his success in that crisis. The most important preparation that the player can make is to decide which crises to avoid. Every crisis, whether won or lost, does some damage. Every crisis poses the risk of an accidental nuclear war. Moreover, every crisis, won or lost, increases the hostility between the superpowers and goads your opponent into more dangerous behavior. The player should refrain from entering crises unless he or she is reasonably confident of success.

The primary skill in crisis management is the judicious assessment of the computer's likely move. If the computer is determined to prevail, then the player should back down immediately. (Better still, the player should never have gotten into the crisis in the first place.) If, on the other hand, the computer's commitment to the issue at stake is weak, then the player should definitely press hard. The problem is that most players have difficulty assessing the computer's likely degree of determination.

There are, of course, the advisors, who present their assessment of the amount of interest of the two superpowers. Unfortunately, their advice is next to useless in the Expert-level game, so you must rely on your own judgment. The only way your judgment can be of any value is if you do your homework before the crisis. This is the "big secret" behind success in *Balance of Power* (as well as in real-world diplomacy): doing your homework.

The first step in doing your homework is to get an overall view of the world situation. This is often very similar to the situation you find in the real world. For example, you can be certain that East Germany will be in the Eastern bloc, and West Germany will be diplomatically very close to the United States. There may be differences of degree in different games, but the rough outlines of the world are the same in all games. Your first task is to find out how the world of *Balance of Power* differs from the real world. To do this, you consult several of the map displays. The Spheres of Influence display is always useful. Any country that is marked as "USA Solid" you can treat as being safely in your sphere and can readily challenge any Soviet intrusion. In the same way, you must keep your nose out of any country shaded as "USSR Solid." Most of your problems will come with the nations between these two extremes.

Before you get into a crisis over such a country, it is a good idea to take the second step and familiarize yourself with the crucial variables that will shape your opponent's behavior in the crisis. Pull down the *Briefing* menu and select "CloseUp" for the country over which a crisis might be fought. There are four things to note in the resulting Closeup window. The first and most important is the Sphere of Influence entry. This will give you a more precise statement of the sphere of influence for that country. If the sphere of influence is "Slightly USSR," you can move with caution. If it is more strongly pro-Soviet than that, you had better not get into any confrontations with the Soviet Union over this country. If it is more favorable to you, you can act with more confidence.

The second item to note in the Closeup window is the country's diplomatic relationships with both superpowers. The critical factor here is not whether or not you are liked, but the relative extremity of the diplomatic relationships. For example, if the country loves you and feels neutral about the Soviets, that puts you in a strong position. However, if the country feels neutral about you and hates the Soviets, then you are in a weak position in a crisis over the country. Why? Because the Soviets feel more strongly than you do about the country and will therefore press their case with more determination than you could.

The third item to note in the Closeup window is the state of treaty relationships between the country and the two superpowers. If your treaty relationship is stronger than that of the Soviets, you are in a better position to press your case in a crisis.

Now fold all three considerations (sphere of influence, diplomatic relations, and treaty) into a single lump. Which superpower has the more pronounced relationship with the country? That superpower will prevail in a crisis. Remember that the computer considers the "outrage excess"—the difference in degree to which the two superpowers are justified in standing firm in a crisis. Even if your claim is weak, you can still prevail if the computer's claim is weaker. Conversely, if your claim is strong, you can still lose if the computer's claim is stronger.

You should do this little homework exercise before challenging the computer over any of its own policies. Too many players read in the newspaper about an action and instantly challenge it. A much wiser policy is to consult the Closeup window for that country before initiating any crisis. Other players engage in fishing expeditions—they challenge the computer "just to see what he'll do." This is a serious mistake. In the first place, every crisis that escalates to the level of a military crisis carries the risk of an accidental nuclear war. Moreover, you lose credibility with your opponent *every* time you back down in a crisis.

There is another side to homework: doing your homework before executing a policy that your opponent might wish to challenge. Before you undertake any provocative action against any questionable country, you should check out its relationships with the superpowers. Make sure that you can get away with it before you try it; to make an attempt and then back down when challenged is worse than doing nothing. If you wish to attempt a risky policy, such as sending weapons to insurgents in Afghanistan, use the old "creeping escalation" trick: Start off with the lowest level of weapons shipments, then increase shipments by one step each turn. Small steps are less inflammatory that big jumps. Over five years you might be able to get away with a policy that you couldn't pull off in a single year.

With your homework done properly, you enter each crisis in the best possible manner: knowing the risks and your opponent's likely behavior. Even so, you must treat each crisis with care. Reject the temptation to mindlessly escalate. There are good reasons to pause at each stage in the crisis and reconsider the merits of continued escalation. In the first place, the amount of prestige at stake will increase each time you escalate. The least you can do is pause to see how much worse you have already made things by escalating to this stage. Much of good statesmanship is having the discipline to avoid being swept up in the passions of the moment. Don't succumb to the temptation to "put it to the floor." That's how most players lose.

There is another reason to pause at each stage of the crisis. The replies that your opponent provides are meaningful and will give you hints as to the likelihood that he will back down. If he is sure of himself and determined to prevail, his language will be tough and assertive, but if he is unsure of his policy, then his language will reflect that uncertainty. Take the time to consider the fine shades of meaning.

Don't be afraid to back down. It hurts to accept defeat, but escalating can only make matters worse if your case is weak. The aphorism to keep in mind is "Cut your losses." You may not win by backing down, but you limit the extent of damage created by a bad move.

There are times when you feel justified in pressing a crisis all the way up to DefCon 2. You just *know* that the computer is bluffing and will back down. If your instincts are correct, then this is the opportunity to make big gains in the game, for there is nothing more productive than winning a big crisis. Pressing your opponent all the way up to DefCon 2 is a high-risk move. If your instincts are correct, you could win the game in a single well-played crisis; if they are wrong, you could just as easily lose the game. If you trust your instincts, go for it. Remember, though, that repeated recourse to high-stakes crises will sooner or later fall victim to the laws of chance. Don't press your luck.

Finally, a player should take care about the order in which he tackles crises. Each turn will present the player with many possible causes over which he might initiate a crisis. The best strategy is to tackle the safest, surest area first, and then move on to the less certain topics. This is because the winner of each crisis gains some *Pugnacity,* which in turn determines the degree to which the other superpower will be intimidated in future crises. This creates something like a diplomatic momentum. Once you have beaten your opponent in one crisis, it is easier to defeat him in the next one. Keep the momentum on your side.

DEALING WITH INSURGENCIES

One of the first tasks facing any player is responding to insurgencies. Insurgencies are the quickest and most dramatic way to change governments around the world. There are two sides to dealing with insurgencies: protecting your friends and overthrowing your enemies.

A great many players see every insurgency as an opportunity that cannot be lost. They feel a need to intervene for one side or the other. What they miss is the fact that some insurgencies are best left alone. (This has been a peculiarly American blind spot since 1960.) You don't have to solve every problem in the world, and if you try, you may well get burned in the process. If you get involved in an insurgency, and your side loses, then you lose prestige. If you attempt to get involved, and your opponent chases you out, then you lose prestige. Thus, there are two prerequisites that must be satisfied before you can commit yourself with success to one side or the other in an insurgency: Your chosen side must be able to win, and you must be able to stare down any crisis challenges.

Can your side win? That depends primarily on the scale of military forces being used in the country. If, for example, the insurgency is a civil war in China, then any resources you could commit would be a drop in the bucket. They would not be able to influence

201

events. If, on the other hand, the insurgency were in Burma, which has no army to speak of, then a very small commitment of resources could easily have a dramatic effect.

A second consideration is the state of the insurgency. In general, once an insurgency has grown by its own efforts to the level of a civil war, any intervention in support of the government is almost a lost cause. If your goal is to support the government, you must take action early and prevent the insurgency from growing to the stage of civil war. Of course, if you have strong treaty commitments to a country, then it may be necessary to take desperate measures to prop up the regime in any way you can. You must not fail to meet your treaty commitments.

On the other hand, if you wish to support the rebels, then it is advantageous to support them even at the last possible minute. In the triumph of victory, the rebels will forget that your fraternal support only came late, and will still regard you as a good friend.

Remember that it is easier to get weapons than troops into a country. Troops are inherently more provocative than weapons, so never try to rush troops into a country without first paving the way with some weapons as a trial balloon. If you manage to bluff your way past the other superpower with the weapons, then you will be able to get the troops in on the next turn. If you try to put in both at once, you could end up with neither, for your opponent will first challenge you on the troops, and then, having forced you to back down, will use the increased sphere of influence he thereby gained to force you to back down on the weapons as well

One difficulty you will have in supporting insurgencies arises from the logistical restrictions on such support. You must infiltrate troops and weapons across the border from a neighboring country. To do this, you must have friendly relations with that neighboring country. This element underscores the importance of maintaining friendly relations with a variety of strategically placed nations. Those few nations will make it possible for you to act against a larger number of neighboring nations.

This suggests one of the long-term strategies possible with *Balance of Power.* If you can identify a likely region for insurgency activity in your favor, such as northeastern Africa (by investigating each of the countries in the region and finding that a majority of these countries are weak, not very favorable to your own country, and struggling against native insurgencies), you can then select the most friendly country in the region to woo as your future base of operations. It takes several turns just to buy enough goodwill with economic and military aid, but perseverance furthers. It will not be possible to force events to move in precisely the path you desire, but it is always worthwhile to develop opportunities.

It is also possible to use insurgencies to tie down your opponent's resources. Both superpowers' supplies of troops and weapons are limited, and some juggling of resources is always necessary. A well-developed insurgency can require a large number of troops to put down if it is primed with enough weapons. For example, a small amount of American weapons sent to the Mujahadeen in Afghanistan could occupy the attention of a large number of Soviet troops. While thus engaged, those troops could not be used elsewhere to intimidate friends or support enemies.

Under no circumstances should you ever send troops into direct combat with your opponent. If the other side has already sent troops to a country, whether for the insurgents or the government, you must refrain from sending your own troops to support the other side. Once Americans and Russians begin killing each other, diplomatic relations between the two countries become poisoned and you will careen from crisis to crisis until the world is destroyed.

COUPS

Coups are not as dramatic as insurgencies in the changes they create. While a revolution can completely change the relationships between countries, a coup has a less marked impact on the state of affairs. Nevertheless, the player should resist coups in friendly nations and encourage them in unfriendly nations. The problem is, when and how?

As with insurgencies, the first mistake that many players make is in getting involved in matters that have little import to them. A coup in an uncommitted country will have little impact on the state of the world. Given the danger of getting into a crisis from which no graceful exit is possible, the wise player tends to avoid entanglements that do not promise real gains. This means that the player should refrain from getting involved in countries that are: (1) neutral, or (2) worth few prestige points. Unless, of course, the player is confident that meddling will be successful.

The primary vehicle for toppling a government with a coup is destabilization. This is not a technique to use heavily—if it fails to topple the government, diplomatic relations will be worsened. It is best to use destabilization only as the last nudge to topple a government already about to fall. This can be determined by consulting the Closeup window for the country. You cannot destroy a government that would otherwise hold up; for all its reputation, the CIA simply cannot invert political realities. Although it can accelerate domestic trends, it doesn't have the power to reverse them. Remember that there is considerable opprobrium associated with destabilization of governments, so again, use restraint with this ugly technique.

There are also indirect strategies for toppling unfriendly governments. Anything you can do to induce the government to increase its military spending will cut into its consumer spending, which will in turn hurt its popularity. How to increase its military spending? Make it feel militarily threatened. Station troops in a neighboring country. Apply diplomatic pressure. Send weapons to the insurgents. All these actions will have the secondary effect of decreasing government stability.

The main way to save a friendly government that is in trouble is to send it economic aid. This is most effective with poor nations and quite useless with wealthy ones. If you act quickly enough, you can save a shaky government with this technique, so long as your opponent does not destabilize the vulnerable government. You may need to go to a crisis to protect your client if this happens.

There are limits to the amount of economic aid that you can send around the world. If you find yourself strapped for foreign aid cash, be sure to reduce the aid that you are sending elsewhere. Reducing foreign aid always generates resentment in the country that is cut off, but if its government is secure, this resentment will be minimal. Your general strategy is thus to take aid away from secure friendly governments and give it to insecure friendly governments.

*F*INLANDIZATION

Finlandization is the most difficult phenomenon to control, but with deliberate strategy you can induce Finlandization in some countries. The basic trick is to make the country feel vulnerable. The first ploy is to station large numbers of your troops in a neighboring country. You don't have to do anything with those troops—their presence alone is menacing enough. Of course, you can't station troops anywhere in the world you please; most nations won't permit it. This is one situation in which the advantage of having good treaty relationships with many countries comes to the fore. Under many treaties, you can freely position troops almost anywhere you wish.

The second ploy is indirect. If you can create an image of ruthlessness, your ability to frighten countries will be enhanced. In other words, if you can make the countries of the world believe that you have no qualms about using your military power, they will be more likely to Finlandize to you. You can foster this image of ruthlessness by intervening frequently and by engaging your opponent in many crises. In other words, you frighten Nicaragua by invading Grenada and talking tough with the Soviets.

There is a danger in this second ploy. Adventurous behavior on your part encourages adventurous behavior on your opponent's part. Throwing your weight around does not make the world more pro-American, it just makes the world more dangerous; and in a dangerous world, small countries behave more deferentially toward large ones. Thus, you must be prepared to cope with a more dangerous adversary should you pursue this second ploy. It is more likely that you will take advantage of the possibilities of this second ploy if the world situation has already deteriorated.

Once you have created the conditions necessary for Finlandization (consult the Closeup window to find out how close your victim is to Finlandizing), apply a judicious amount of diplomatic pressure to throw your victim over the brink. Do not apply too much or you will only instigate a challenge from your opponent. Use just enough to produce the desired Finlandization. How much is that? Consult the Closeup window and make an educated guess.

If you are successful, be prepared to follow up with further action. Your victim might repudiate any treaties it has with your opponent—rush in to offer a security treaty of your own. Offer economic assistance or weapons shipments, anything to consolidate your position with the government.

Your best defense against an opponent's attempts to intimidate your clients is your integrity coupled with treaty commitments. Offer treaties to clients that you think are vulnerable, but only if you believe you can honor those commitments. It would be a terrible mistake to sign a treaty with a government that is losing a civil war; you would be almost certain to lose integrity when the government fell.

Another way to bolster the confidence of a fearful client is to station troops there. Your troops will increase the sense of security of the client. You could also send it more weapons for its army; this is especially effective with poor countries that have large but ill-equipped armies. A small amount of weaponry will greatly increase the overall effectiveness of the army and the government's sense of security.

This does suggest a valuable indirect strategy toward Finlandization. If you ever get an opportunity to overthrow a government to which your opponent has strong commitments, press the opportunity for all it's worth; if you succeed, you will win more than just the single country. The destruction of your opponent's integrity will make it easier to induce his clients to Finlandize to you.

*P*LAYING AS THE USSR

Most people play *Balance of Power* as the United States, and so do not appreciate the special problems of the Soviet Union. You should try playing as the USSR some time to develop a better feel for Soviet paranoia. As the General Secretary of the USSR, you will find that your resources are more limited than those of the American President. More important, you will find that you have fewer friends around the world. In fact, the world looks quite hostile from Moscow. Outside of Eastern Europe, your only friends are Cuba, Nicaragua, Ethiopia, Angola, North Korea, Afghanistan, and Vietnam. This is not a very impressive list. Nicaragua is quite vulnerable to Yankee adventurism, and it is normally best to write it off as a lost cause, but you might be able to at least keep the Americans occupied with the place before losing it.

Ethiopia is always vulnerable, but can also be vital for expansion into Africa. Angola is in much the same position. Pursue your African openings with all possible vigor, for the Americans have little influence there and the local governments are easily manipulated with the smaller amounts of resources available to you. Vietnam can be used as a springboard against Thailand, although the Americans can easily block this.

The Americans' greatest vulnerability is the extent of their connections around the world. They have so many friends that they cannot possibly stretch their resources to cover all of them; if you can find the chink in the American system, the one or two American clients that are vulnerable to insurgency or a coup or Finlandization, you can discredit American prestige by toppling these clients. This can trigger a loss of confidence in American treaties that may induce a stampede of Finlandization toward you. This implies that a more unstable world is often to your advantage.

GENERAL COMMENTS

Most players are too impatient and too adventurous. This is a game of power politics and diplomacy, and you cannot win by playing cowboy. You must be circumspect. You must learn the skills of the diplomat. It is painful to swallow your pride and take your losses, but this is the only way to win.

Remember, this game lasts for eight years. Don't try to win it all in the first year. Most players last only two years before they blow up the world. Exercise restraint and slowly, patiently develop your plans. It's better to go for long-term victories rather than short-term conquests.

Although the game does emphasize the brutal realities of power politics, you must not abandon your sense of moral restraint. *Balance of Power* includes a great many checks against flagrant violations of the moral sensibilities of mankind. If you ignore your treaty commitments, your clients will Finlandize to your opponent. Whenever you take any action against any government, you increase the level of barbarism in the world, which only encourages your opponent to behave in a similar fashion. Whenever you worsen relations with your opponent, you increase the chance that a crisis will trigger an accidental nuclear war. A civilized statesman cannot be a saint, but he must not be a barbarian.

Finally, you must recognize that, in the world of power politics, there are never any big winners. The diplomat never visualizes himself triumphant, standing with his foot on the neck of his groveling defeated foe, fist raised high to the adulation of the crowd. In a world with nuclear weapons, there can never be any such thing as total victory. There can only be small victories—or total defeat.

HOW BALANCE OF POWER WAS CREATED

The explanation of *Balance of Power* presented in this book has a neat and tidy appearance. One might easily get the impression that the creation of the game was a straight-forward exercise, a simple matter of sitting down in front of the computer and transferring the information presented in these pages to the computer. The true situation is more like that of the diver who, when asked by the sportswriter, "How did you manage to execute a double Fournier backtwister coming out of a swan dive?", answers, "I don't remember anything after my foot slipped on the edge of the board."

The process of creating *Balance of Power* was likewise a series of desperate midair thrashings whose outcome has a deceptive elegance. I had, of course, a guiding sense throughout the process, but a great many of the most important decisions were made for the most unlikely reasons. Now that it is all over, I would like to be able to say "I planned it that way," but that is not true. In this chapter, I hope to present a chronological explanation of how *Balance of Power* came to be. This might instill a greater sense of sympathy in the reader for the travails of game design, as well as some insight into the design process itself.

One last prefatory comment: The concepts behind the game evolved with time. That is, I did not start out with a fixed set of notions and then express those notions directly through the computer. Instead, the attempt to express my thoughts on the problems of geopolitics helped refine and correct them. One of my English teachers used to badger me with the slogan, "If you can't say it, you don't know it!" His slogan is also applicable to a programmer. As long as you are basically literate in programming, you should be able to express any logical relationship you understand. It therefore follows that any logical relationship you cannot express, you do not understand. I have found that this principle can be turned around: If you don't understand a logical relationship, you can use the attempt to program it as a means to learn about it. So it was with *Balance of Power.* As I worked on the game, my understanding of geopolitics improved and my improved understanding was incorporated into the game.

PREHISTORY

The seeds that would lead to *Balance of Power* were planted in 1966 and 1968. The first was planted by a high school friend who introduced me to commercial wargames. I took a liking to the games, but they remained a minor interest for seven years. The second seed was planted when my father let me play with the computer at his job; I had a lot of fun but, again, did not devote myself to the study of this strange machine. During my undergraduate years I dabbled occasionally in both wargames and computers, the first for fun, the second for school-work in physics.

It was at graduate school that two chance events rekindled the flames. I happened to run across a copy of *Strategy and Tactics*, a magazine that discussed the history behind the wargames. I was fascinated—the wargames I had played suddenly took on a new meaning to me. I resumed playing them, and began studying the history of war with renewed energy.

The second event came just a few months later. I ran into a fellow at the university computer center who was writing a program that would play a wargame. The very notion flabbergasted me: How could anybody hope to write a program to handle the myriad problems of wargame play? I could not take the fellow seriously.

By the time I received my master's degree in physics, I had a consuming passion for computers, wargames, and the history of war. I took a job teaching physics and pursued all three interests. I tackled the problem of programming a computer to play a wargame, and surprised myself by getting a working game running on the school's tiny IBM 1130 computer after only six months' effort. I first showed it to other wargamers in December, 1976. It was, to my knowledge, the first recreational computer wargame.

It was also at this time that I first became aware of microcomputers. I was immediately obsessed by the notion of owning my very own computer, and in January of 1977 I realized my dream with the purchase of a KIM-1 single-board computer with a 6502 processor and 1K of RAM. I taught myself machine language and had my first game running in a month. Over the next twenty months I expanded my system and developed a wargame for the machine.

Then in September, 1978, I purchased a Commodore PET computer and began redesigning my wargame to run on the PET. I sold my first copy of the game, called *Tanktics*, on December 31, 1978. I developed another wargame, called *Legionnaire*, in early 1979. But I was already beginning to tire of simple wargames; I wanted to design a game about the larger problems of war and peace, not just the mechanics of warfare.

*E*ARLY ATTEMPTS

My first attempt at a game modeling geopolitics was made in July, 1979. The game was called *Policy*. What I had in mind was a strategic wargame in which wars were meant to be minor. There would be a number of combatants, and no one would have the resources to fight a total war. Instead, wars would be small, localized affairs aimed at weakening an opponent or seizing some territory. The target machine was a Commodore PET with 8K of RAM, and most of the program would be written in BASIC. I worked on the game for only a month and got a portion of it running. Then I realized that it was fundamentally flawed:

It had evolved into a strategic resource-management game. You spent most of your time in the game just shuffling around your resources. The game's architecture didn't support its point. I set it aside while I handled the problems of moving to Silicon Valley for my wife's new job. The next thing I knew, I was working at Atari, and *Policy* was shelved for good.

While at Atari I worked on a variety of simple games. The marketing experts at Atari were confident that no game so complex as a wargame, much less anything like *Policy,* could ever attract much of a market. For two years I worked on a variety of other projects. Then in December, 1981, Dr. Alan Kay hired me into his Corporate Research Group at Atari with a mission of creating original new games. I set to work on a grand game based on the Arthurian legends; that effort consumed eighteen months of my time and resulted in *Excalibur.*

One year later I was able to hire a new programmer to work on a new game, and I was determined to return to the geopolitical theme that I had attempted with *Policy.* However, this time I had much grander goals. In the first place, I set as the target machine an Atari 800 with 48K of RAM and a disk drive, programmed in assembly language. This was a machine with considerably more horsepower than the first, and my plans were suitably grander. In the interim, I had read Henry Kissinger's *White House Years* and was impressed with the complexity of modern diplomacy. My goal with this game was (to quote a design document prepared during planning) "to teach people about the intricacies of the arms race." The emphasis on this game was weapons development and deployment. The options available to the player included such complex things as ABM systems, Civil

217

Defense programs, ICBMs, cruise missiles, satellite weapons, and so forth. You could also sign treaties to prevent deployment of such systems, or dismantle existing ones. Initially, the basic idea of the game was to come up with a mix of weapons systems good enough to deter a Soviet attack yet somehow pursue an arms control strategy that would keep your country from going bankrupt. We spent a great deal of time trying to work out the details, but could not seem to come up with a balanced design. Later on, we decided to make the game more theoretical in style, with only seven nations, and four dimensions of interplay between them: trade, weapons sales, treaties, and public relations. The game was beginning to take form when the programmer lost interest in the project, and I eventually assigned her to another project.

As luck would have it, barely six months passed before I had another opportunity to try again with my "peacegame." Another group at Atari was developing a bulletin board system and wanted a game for the system. A deal was made: They would supply the programmer if I would supply the design expertise. As it happened, the person assigned was a good friend of mine who was also knowledgeable about games. So I set to work designing a multi-player game of international conflict. We agreed that this would not be a "conquer the world" game, as some telecommunications games had become. Instead, we imagined a game of geopolitical conflict, with a great deal of negotiation going on between the parties and a very small amount of military conflict. Unfortunately, the collapse of Atari led to the programmer's being laid off before serious work could commence.

THE GENESIS OF ARMS RACE

Three times I had begun work on my game of geopolitical interaction; three times the project had fallen apart. On March 16, 1984, I was laid off from Atari. It was time to define a new project. I had followed the introduction of Apple's Macintosh computer with great interest and quickly resolved that my next game would be designed for this machine, which I viewed as a game designer's dream—lots of horsepower and a well-defined and expressive user interface. On April 6, 1984, I sent a letter to a software publishing house presenting a list of games for discussion. Among the games on the list was one called *Arms Race.* The one-paragraph description said:

> *Negotiate the treaties that will decide the fate of humanity. Your Russian opponent is hard to fathom. Is he a reasonable person sincerely seeking an end to this desperate race? Is he motivated by fear or by greed? Can you trust him? How do the new technologies of mass destruction change things? This game will focus more on geopolitics than on the arms race itself. I intend to show that good men can still annihilate the world through miscalculation. The game would show superpower conflict through the small countries, demonstrating that these proxy wars are the most likely trigger for Armageddon. This game will probably include every country in the world, with lots of relationships between them . . . .*

Here is *Balance of Power* for the first time. In the three previous versions I had struggled with a variety of ideas, among them resource management, weapons development, and multi-player concerns—but this was the first statement that captured the essence of what was to become the final game. Note the reference to "new technologies of mass destruction," as well as the title itself. I couldn't quite shake free from weapons development as a subject for a game.

Only three weeks later, the idea had developed considerably. In a letter to my agent, Steve Axelrod, I described the game as follows:

> *This is . . . the game that I have been wanting to do for a long time. I propose a game that shows why the USA and the Soviet Union are locked in a dangerous balance of terror. You are the President for the entire 40-year span of the game (1960-2000). All you have to do is get to the turn of the century without igniting Armageddon. It's not easy. The game is actually about geopolitics, not the arms race per se. You are tied into numerous alliances with small countries the world over. This complex web of obligations is constantly being strained by the petty disputes of the small countries. These small squabbles can erupt into war at any time, and the danger always exists that events could suck you into a major confrontation with the Soviet Union. The central question of the game, then, is to ask how the US and the USSR can carry on a global rivalry without eventually getting themselves into a nuclear war. The answer, of course, is that they can do so only by rigorously constraining and reducing the scope of that conflict.*
>
> *The game would use a smart map that presents a great deal of information about nations and their relationships in graphical format. Icons would show treaty relations, military status, bases, and so forth . . . . I think that this game would grab a great deal of attention.*

In just three weeks, the game had come a long way. There were still some misconceptions in this description, the most notable being the idea that confrontations would be caused by wars between minor countries. (What I had in mind was the Yom Kippur War of 1973.) This feature played a large role in my thinking until very late in the development of the game.

In early May, 1984, I decided that *Arms Race* was my next project and set to work gathering references and organizing my thoughts. Realizing the difficulty of the task before me, I wrote down my thoughts as I developed them. Now that the game is complete, these notes give testimony to the many dead ends and blind spots that arise during the course of the design process. Thus, on May 14, I wrote:

> *What about issues such as credibility, moral leadership, idealism and cynicism, resolve, confidence, and trustworthiness? How are these quantities expressed, recorded, and maintained?*

As it happens, only one of these variables (*trustworthiness*, which became *Integrity*) eventually made it into the game; oddly enough, the very next sentence captures the scheme that I eventually hit upon:

> *If you are supporting a country, and the USSR gives aid to the insurgents, and you don't respond quickly enough, other countries will lose faith in you.*

Later on, I added a question that players of *Balance of Power* will instantly recognize:

Can we embellish events with news stories with some color, perhaps using a sentence generator? This would make events seem more natural.

On the other hand, there were plenty of blind alleys. One idea I wanted was an endgame analysis that would critique the player's performance, suggesting things such as, "Your weakness in the face of Russian aggression encouraged further adventures and disheartened your allies." I had no idea how I would implement this feature, but it sure sounded nice.

Then there were problems of scale. I initially decided to have each turn of the game represent one month of time. This, coupled with the 10-year game span that I had by now settled on, implied a game with 120 turns to it! I did not realize at the time how long each turn would take, so I pressed ahead. This turned out to be one of the most bedeviling problems in the game design process. As I realized that the game took too long to play, I kept chopping down on the number of turns, first going to turns that were one year long, then going to games that were fifteen years, then ten years, and finally eight years.

Two other documents from the first month illustrate two of the problems of game design. The first and more trivial concerned the working title of the game. Consumers may not realize that very few games actually reach the market with the title that was originally chosen by the author. For some reason game designers make lousy title-pickers. Of my seven published games, only two were published under the original working title. All of the others were given new titles just before shipment. For example, *Ourrah Pobieda* was retitled

Eastern Front (1941) and *Three Mile Island* became *Scram*. In May, 1984, I considered a number of possible titles: *Annihilation of Mankind, The Extension of Policy,* and *Thwarting Armageddon.* I finally settled on *Arms Race.* The game was designed with this title in mind. (Resourceful players who rummage around with the files on the disk can find a number of vestiges of this old title.) The final title, *Balance of Power,* was suggested by Roger Buoy of Mindscape (along with such alternatives as *That's the Way the Planet Crumbles*) and it immediately stuck. It is, after all, a better title.

The more substantive issue was the nature of the verbs that would be provided in the game. Verbs are all-important in game design. They are the allowed actions, the permissible commands that are available to the player. A good set of verbs allows players to do everything they would need or want to do. A poor set of verbs will either confuse them with its arbitrariness, or lock them in a frustrating straitjacket. The game designer spends a great deal of design effort worrying about the verbs to provide in the game. Thus, on May 11, I wrote down my list of intended verbs. It is longer than the eight verbs allowed in the final version of the game, yet not as clean or understandable. The verbs in the final version of the game fit together well, covering all the bases very simply and powerfully. One would not have believed that such a clean set of verbs could have evolved from the almost random list I first drew up. Here is that list:

Provide arms to insurgents
Provide shelter to insurgents
Give economic aid
Give military aid

Allow weapons sales
Apply trade embargo
Intervene
Offer mutual defense treaty
Go to summit meeting
Set military spending level
Make military demonstration (attempt to intimidate)
Declare war
Blockade
Establish or break diplomatic relations
Set level of rhetoric

The italicized entries were the only ones that made it into the final game. All the others fell by the wayside during the course of development. It is a sad truth that most game designers aim high and always hit a little lower than they had intended.

Another effort during those early days was research. I collected every book on world affairs that I could find. The fascinating maps in *The War Atlas* (Kidron and Smith 1983) inspired me to emphasize a graphics-intensive display. I thought I had struck gold when I found a book entitled *The War Trap* (Bueno de Mesquita 1981). Here was a complete, mathematically expressed theory for the genesis of wars. It seemed that all I needed to do was program in the professor's formulas, plug in some data, and I would have my game. Further study, though, disabused me of that idea. His work was very interesting but not quite germane to the goals of my game. It was reassuring, though, to know that somebody else had seriously attempted to express geopolitical interactions in mathematical terms. At least I wasn't alone in the effort.

In June, I started writing little essays to myself on various aspects of the game. The purpose of these essays was to help me organize my thoughts on the game. In some of them I cut loose and dreamed grand things; in others I carefully plotted the details of bits and bytes that would be necessary to make the program run. It was during this time that I hit upon the central scheme that every government in the world would have its very own insurgency to bedevil it. However, I got a little carried away with this idea. First, I intended to have insurgency measured in terms of its military strength (this showed up in the final game) and also its popular support (this didn't). Moreover, the government would be rated for its oppressiveness as well as its own popular support.

These essays helped me define many of the internal details of the game. Concepts such as diplomatic affinity, commitment, and credibility first appeared in these essays. More important, the essays helped me clarify my own thinking on the central problems of the design. Because of them, I was able to make tough design decisions with a clearer understanding of my priorities.

Based on all these considerations, I put together a proposal in early July. My agent was attempting to sell the game to publishers, who need a detailed proposal on which to base their considerations. The proposal was some fourteen single-spaced pages long, and describes the final product fairly well. One idea included in the proposal that failed to make it into the final product was the "rubber map graphic." My intention here was to allow a player to select some variable, such as GNP, and watch the map distort so that the area of each country would be proportional to its GNP. Unfortunately, I was unable to derive an algorithm that would execute the rubber map graphic quickly enough, so I had to settle for the shading system used in the final product. Many people do not realize how many ideas must be tried, worked on, and discarded before the final product is defined.

I spent a good deal of space in that proposal attempting to address the problems of political bias and my own political goals in the game. The most important statements in this section were: "This game will reject the notion that war is the product of evil men with hearts of hate . . . . It will instead attempt to demonstrate that good men with good intentions can trap themselves in a situation from which war is inescapable." This was a fundamental goal of the game, one to which I adhered throughout the long development cycle. I very much wanted to make people question their sense of moral superiority over leaders who get into wars. Maintaininng peace takes foresight and wisdom, not merely good intentions.

On the all-important question of verbs, this proposal had whittled the verb count down to ten:

Set military spending
Set consumer spending
Set trade access of another country
Provide arms to insurgents
Offer economic aid
Offer military aid
Intervene
Offer mutual defense treaty
Declare war
Declare diplomatic warmth

Again, italics indicate verbs that made it into the final game. As you can see, I was zeroing in on the final verb set.

The last interesting item in this proposal, written in July, 1984, was the schedule. I projected a working version of the game by January 1, 1985, with final, tested, polished code ready on May 1, 1985. As is common with software proposals, this projection turned out to be optimistic.

PROGRAMMING BEGINS

During this time I had been designing without programming. I had a Macintosh but no development system for the Mac. In those days, the only way to develop serious Macintosh programs was on a Lisa computer. I had ordered a Lisa from Apple in May, 1984, but I did not receive the machine until August 1. So I spent the first three months of the project doing "paper design." Without a development system, all I could do was read the manuals, study my references, and write proposals. As it happens, this can be a good thing . . . if it does not go on for too long. Too many games are hacked together at the keyboard rather than designed from the ground up. In this case, however, three months of paper design was too long because during the process I needed to test some ideas on the computer before I could proceed with other aspects of the design. It was with great relief that I took delivery of my Lisa and set to work learning the system.

Many observers have commented on the difficulty that programmers seem to have learning how to make the most of the Mac. A common excuse for the dearth of software early in the machine's life is the difficulty that programmers experienced in coming up to speed on the Mac. I did not experience such difficulties. True, I was intimidated by the complexity of the machine, but I was programming comfortably within a month. I suspect that the main reason for the delays so many programmers experienced with the Mac was the desire of the typical programmer to understand all aspects of the machine before undertaking a project. I was not so fastidious. My heavy use of MacWrite and MacPaint had given me a feeling for the machine's capabilities—that was enough to get started. I plunged into the programming effort with wild abandon, learning only those features that I needed to know to solve a particular problem. This approach gets the job at hand done, but it can leave gaping holes in a programmer's repertoire. Even today, two years after I started working with the Mac, I buttonhole other programmers with stupid questions about fundamentals of Macintosh programming. I am fortunate that *other* programmers took the time to learn all those tiresome details that I rushed past in my hurry to get the game done, and were then patient enough to explain their hard-won understanding to me.

Because so much of the game revolves around it, my first task was the creation of the map:

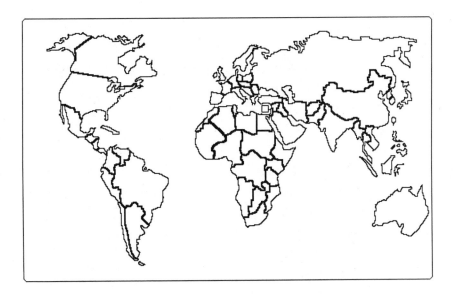

My solution to this problem is an object case in design philosophy. You can see that it is indeed an intricate representation of the world. How, people ask me, did I digitize it? My answer drops jaws: I did it by hand. I started with a map of the world, which I traced freehand onto graph paper. I then redrew the lines to conform to the rectangular grid of the graph paper. I then scaled up the map to be more appropriate to the Mac's screen. This rescaling was non-integral, so I did it by hand again, estimating rescaling values for each line segment. Some fudging here and there gave me the final map, represented on some two dozen sheets of graph paper. The only task remaining was to get it into the computer. I sat down with a tape recorder and started reading coordinates from the graph paper: "Nigeria. Origin at X = 138, Y= 227. One step north, 1 east, 2 north, 3 east ..."

Then I sat at the computer and replayed the tape, typing in the values as they came tumbling off the tape. The string of directional steps marking the course of the border was translated into a compact sequence of numerals and single letters, like so: NE2N3E. I then wrote routines that converted these strings into the graphic representations of the countries.

Experienced programmers will shake their heads in dismay at this method. Surely there is some easier way to have done the work, some tool that would have made the effort go much faster. Undoubtedly there is. Here is where design philosophy comes in. A programming tool is like a freeway: It takes you somewhere in the universe of results. All programming tools are to some extent generalized to handle the needs of a large number of programmers. They are like freeways that take you to the most popular beaches or the most crowded resorts. He who would climb the remote peaks must forsake the comfort of the freeway and make his way by foot. The exertion of a week's simple sweat can place the programmer on a mountain peak from which are visible new territories of creative opportunity invisible to those who veer away from steep grades.

During October I made one of the first painful deletions in the game: I removed all references to trade between nations. I had originally intended to have trade play a major part in the game. As I saw it, trade would play a large role in determining the rate of growth of each country's GNP. Thus, each nation would want to maximize its foreign trade. This would make trade embargoes a useful weapon of geopolitical competition. I had therefore carefully researched the amount of trade between all the nations of the world. This information was compiled on a huge sheet of graph paper, with the total amount of trade between each of the 3,844 pairs of nations in my game recorded in the appropriate square on the graph paper. I then entered all that data into the program. Unfortunately, a huge array of this nature eats up a lot of RAM; in this case, some 7,688 bytes were necessary to record trade. As early as October I ran out of RAM. Realizing that I would be needing far more RAM, I decided that something had to be eliminated from the program. Trade was the obvious target since its removal would free up a great deal of RAM in a single stroke.

This episode illustrates another murderous problem in game design: the need to balance resources in pursuit of the goal. A game designer has four finite expendable resources to bring to the game: RAM, disk space, the microprocessor's execution time, and his own time. Almost every game design decision must take into account the impact of the various options on these precious resources. Sad to say, almost every desirable feature eats up large quantities of all resources. The beginning game designer often views game design as a feast at a table heaped with all manner of potential features; the hardened veteran thinks more in terms of a trek across a desert with limited quantities of food, water, and equipment.

All through September, October, and November I ground out the code. Apparently the three months I spent waiting for my development system gave me the opportunity to organize my thoughts so well that I was able to work very quickly once I did have my development system. By mid-November I had a working program that included many of the features of the final *Balance of Power*, yet remained in a formative stage. It was like a duckling who has the bill, webbed feet, and general conformation of the adult duck but is still far less than an adult duck. So, too, the November version of the game was recognizable but fell short of final product. It couldn't even waddle.

MARKETING PROBLEMS

It was about this time that I realized that I was in serious financial trouble. The cataclysmic destruction of the entertainment software industry was just gathering momentum in early 1984, and would not peak until late 1984. Publishers who had seriously intended to do business with me in May were no longer in business in October. My agent and I had been confident that we could sell the *Arms Race* proposal by August. August came and went with no buyers. Other business proposals were equally fruitless. By November I was running out of money and had no prospective buyers for the game. Facing bankruptcy, I decided to compress the development cycle and wrap up the game in an unpublishable state by January 1. I didn't know what I would do then, but there seemed little point in continuing a hopeless effort. I was ready to give up.

At this point Jim Warren intervened. Jim had founded the West Coast Computer Faire in the mid-seventies and played a pivotal role in getting the microcomputer revolution off the ground. His technical expertise, easygoing good humor, and sense of community are legendary in the microcomputer world. He had learned through friends that I was working on a grand, idealistic game about peace and war but was in financial trouble. He invited me up to his beautiful house in the Santa Cruz mountains, where we talked about my problems. Jim urged me to stick with the game. His encouragement and optimism inspired me to pick up the gauntlet again. Maybe it was the fresh mountain air, but I left that meeting thinking that I could somehow overcome all problems. Jim Warren saved *Balance of Power*.

*S*ERENDIPITY

In the midst of all these difficulties I came up with the single grand stroke that transformed the game: the crisis. My written notes from the time are sketchy; I was in the midst of one of those fevered brainstorms that does not admit time for pause. The crisis was initially created as a stopgap measure to solve the following problem: How do we prevent a superpower from pursuing an obviously outrageous policy? For example, what is to prevent the USA from invading East Germany, or the USSR from invading Mexico? These are ridiculous policy options that no sane superpower would ever pursue, but this is a game, and players *will* attempt such things. What's to stop them?

My quick and dirty solution was to allow any country to deplore any other country's actions. My original intent had been that deploring would be little more than posturing, a way to stimulate international condemnation and consequent loss of prestige for a particularly outrageous action. Somewhere I got the notion that the offending party should have the opportunity to reconsider its action and reverse the policy. From there it was only a short step to the concept of the escalating crisis, with each party alternating in its consideration of whether to escalate or back down. And from there the addition of DefCon 1 and the consequent loss of the game added a tremendous boost to the excitement and intensity of play. Of course, there was still a great deal of work required to make the crisis work neatly. I continued to polish the crisis segment of the game right up the very end of the development cycle.

It is my duty to admit that this, the most important single feature of the game, was *never* mentioned in any of my planning documents. For all my advocacy of careful design and maintenance of purpose, I have to admit that this was just a stroke of luck. These things happen. The seasoned game designer does not embark on a project expecting a brainstorm halfway through to make the game. Careful design and planning make good games; the addition of a lucky stroke of genius, developed masterfully, makes great games.

*T*HE *RANDOM HOUSE INTERLUDE*

The outlook for the game took a dramatic turn for the better just before Thanksgiving, 1984. Random House expressed interest in publishing the game. Negotiations proceeded during December, with a senior official from Random House visiting me twice to discuss the game and my plans for further enhancements and modifications to it. In January, 1985, we signed a contract calling for a March 1 delivery of the game. It was foolish of me to promise so early a delivery on a game that I had originally scheduled for a May 1 delivery, but I was desperate. I resolved to work long hours and make the deadline. And indeed, my progress during January and February was phenomenal. I put in the title page with its unique dissolving images and a variety of additional features: two-player games, ability to play either as the USA or the USSR, four levels of play, and the ability to save and load the game. I greatly refined the operation of the crisis and put in the first artificial intelligence routines to operate the other countries. I worked killing hours trying to meet that deadline, but by mid-February it was obvious to me that I would not make deadline. I so informed Random House, and they were gracious; their only concern was the quality of the product.

During March, I labored with the artificial intelligence routines. I also added the Background and Closeup features, and nailed down the final set of eight verbs that appears in the published version of the game.

At this time, Random House assigned an editor to the project to take over the final details of the game. This editor studied the game and prepared a list of criticisms and suggestions for the game. For the next few weeks I struggled to implement those features suggested by the new editor as well as those I knew needed inclusion. However, it soon became obvious that we had serious disagreements over the project. I was under the impression that the game was in the final stages before release, and the editor seemed to think that it needed major modifications. Despite our deep differences, we were able to hammer out an agreement specifying a series of changes that I would make to the game. I spent three weeks implementing most of these changes. The two most important of these changes were the History feature and the advisors' commentary during a crisis. I was very pleased with the result, and thought that I was in a strong position. After all, the game was much better than I had promised it would be, I had worked far longer than I had promised, I had responded positively to almost all of Random House's demands, and I knew that the game was just plain great. I therefore presented the result to Random House with an ultimatum: Accept this version as the alpha-test version of the game, or drop the contract. Random House opted to drop the contract. Oops!

METTLE-TESTING

It was now early May, 1985. I was without a contract and in debt to Random House for the money that had already been advanced. Facing bankruptcy, I started looking for what my wife called "a *real* job." I was hoping that somehow, some publisher would change its mind and publish the game, but it looked hopeless at this stage. There was no money left to allow me to finish it. I would work on it until I got a job, and then abandon it. Until then, my highest priority had to be finding a job.

My agent raced to sell the game to any publisher who would cover my debt to Random House. But nobody wanted this game. They all admired it, said that it was beautiful, but not worth what we had to ask for in advance money. The rejection notices piled up; it seemed a sad ending to such a noble effort.

The tremendous strain of this period began to take its toll. After a year's effort and so many rejections, I was just about at the end of my tether.

I continued to polish the game. The greatest change during this period was the final "lobotomization of the minor countries." My initial design of *Arms Race* was completely nonpolar. There was no fundamental difference in the program between the USA and any other country. Every country had the same policy options available to it that were available to the superpowers. But this egalitarian view of the world was slowly transformed during the development process. First came the crisis, which allowed the superpowers (but no other country) to start a crisis and carry it through to a nuclear war. Later, I made some further changes to cut down on the amount of activity that non-superpowers could undertake. By May, there was only one policy option left to the non-superpowers: the right to declare war on another non-superpower.

I had been spreading the game among playtesters and was getting unanimous feedback that the game was too difficult to understand. The major complaint seemed to be that there was too much activity to occupy the attentions of the player. The uncontrollable activities of the non-superpowers seemed to be a big part of the problem. Players felt helpless in a world in which so many things took place outside their control. The game should have felt like high noon on main street of a dusty Western town, with the player squaring off for the final showdown with Gorbachev; instead, the game played like Saturday night at the saloon, with everybody behind tables, shooting it out, and the player standing in the middle shouting, "What's going on?"

I took much pride in the multipolarity of the game; it is, after all, a very realistic representation of the world. However, one ignores one's playtesters at one's own peril, so with great reluctance I finally lobotomized the minor countries, reducing them to passive pawns to be manipulated by the superpowers. The accessibility of the game took a giant leap.

Another playtester unwittingly contributed one of the nicest touches in the game: the black endgame screen that announces, "You have ignited a thermonuclear war. And no, there is no animated display of a mushroom cloud with parts of bodies flying through the air. We do not reward failure." The text for this display was my own creation. I had cooked it up sometime in February of 1985 in a disgusted reaction to the question of a friend who wanted to know if I would be putting in some great graphics for the end of the world. However, my original rendition had placed the text in a nondescript Macintosh window that presented its message with all the panache of a bus driver announcing the bus's arrival at the next stop. I happened to be on hand one day as a playtester explained the game to his friend. In describing the end of the game, he mistakenly claimed that the screen went black before the final message appeared. I started to correct him, then bit my tongue. What a great idea! Four hours later the playtester's mistake was my newest feature.

One of the oddities of this world is the way in which seemingly insignificant events can lead to major changes. In March, 1985, I had been asked to speak to a local meeting of the Macintosh Special Interest Group of the Software Entrepreneurs' Forum about game software. This is a very small group; perhaps thirty people attended the meeting at which I spoke. One of them, however, was Steve Jasik, who suggested to the speaker coordinator of the Berkeley Macintosh Users Group that I might make a good speaker for that group. I ended up showing my game and giving a speech to the group in early May, 1985. Attending that meeting was Tom Maremaa, a reporter for the computer magazine *InfoWorld*. Tom was impressed with *Arms Race* and later interviewed me and wrote an article that appeared in the June 10, 1985, issue of *InfoWorld*. The effect was electric. Software publishers called from all over the country to express interest in the game. One of the publishers who saw the article and approached my agent was Mindscape. After some telephone discussion, the principles for a contract were agreed to.

A few days later I flew out to Chicago to meet with the Mindscape people and discuss final changes in the game. That meeting was a model for the proper relationship between artist and publisher. It was chaired by Sandy Schneider, the most talented editorial worker I have ever encountered. We went over every detail of the game in six hours. The Mindscape people brought a long list of suggested changes. Each item was read off and discussed by all concerned. There was no idle brainstorming, no random ruminations; Sandy kept the meeting moving. The arguments in favor of, or opposed to, a point were presented concisely and forcefully. A few minutes of discussion sufficed to generate a consensus. Notes were taken and we moved on to the next suggestion.

During July, I made the changes agreed to at the meeting. Most of the changes were minor matters of polishing. For example, I reduced the probability of accidental nuclear war. Other changes made the user interface smoother and simpler. On August 1, 1985, I turned over semi-final code to Mindscape for testing. After seven weeks of testing, about a dozen bugs had been found and corrected. The best bug report was the observation that the capital of Tanzania is spelled "Dar es Salaam," not "Dar Es Salaam." These testers were thorough. I turned in the final version of the game in late September and *Balance of Power* was finished. The first production copies were shipped in mid-October.

AFTERTHOUGHTS

The development of *Balance of Power* reminds me of the use of paratroops in World War II. After much trial and error, the strategists eventually learned that the real value of paratroops lay in their power to motivate regular troops to fight to rescue the paratroops. It's difficult to inspire soldiers to risk their lives to win a patch of ground, but when they know that their comrades are just ahead, surrounded by the enemy, counting on the regular troops to save them, the regular troops will fight with unparalleled determination. Paratroops, then, allow the commander to set a clear and tough goal for his troops to reach. Using paratroops is like putting yourself in a deep hole to see if you can dig yourself out of it.

I did much the same thing with *Balance of Power*, setting a goal for myself that I had no reason to believe I could attain. Then I publicly and financially committed myself to attaining that goal. Nobody believed that I could do it, certainly not any publishers. The thought that I could design a game on geopolitics that would be interesting, challenging, understandable, and fun was just not credible to them. Having dug this deep hole for myself, I then started digging myself out. Several times the walls caved in on me, leaving just one free hand groping madly for air. It was a tough, frightening experience. When it was over I was physically and spiritually spent. But what is the point of undertaking anything less than the most demanding of efforts?

APPENDIX: A SAMPLE
EXPERT-LEVEL GAME

This appendix was written to serve two needs: to provide a more complete representation of the game *Balance of Power* for those who have not had the pleasure of playing it, and to provide instruction by example for those who have difficulty winning the game even after reading the theoretical material in the book.

To prepare this Appendix, I sat down with a Macintosh, fired up *Balance of Power,* and played a sample game. This sample game differs from a regular game in two ways. First, I had to frequently interrupt play to take notes for this Appendix and send screen shots to the disk. Second, I played more carefully and thoroughly than I normally do. It would be very embarrassing to set out to play a sample game and *lose!* Even for me, the designer, winning takes careful, thoughtful play. But the fact that I could sit down to play with the expectation of winning should indicate my confidence in the belief that *Balance of Power* is a game that can be mastered.

My approach in this Appendix is to present my thoughts on the game as it unfolds. This should give the reader a better idea of the thinking processes that go on during play than would be obtained by presenting a sanitized version of my actions. Thus, my mistakes will be evident as well as my successes. I also include afterthoughts made upon completion of the game that point out my miscalculations.

In the following discussion, I sometimes use the verb "destabilize." This verb refers to the policy of destabilization found on the *Make Policies* menu under the menu item "Destabilize."

TURN 1: 1986

I begin by taking a few minutes to familiarize myself with the world situation. The Major Events display shows revolutions in Mali, Zaire, Mozambique, and Burma. I check out some fundamental displays: Insurgency, Spheres of Influence, Diplomatic Relations for both superpowers, Likelihood of a Coup d'Etat, and the two displays showing likelihood of Finlandizing. Of these, the Insurgency display is the most important:

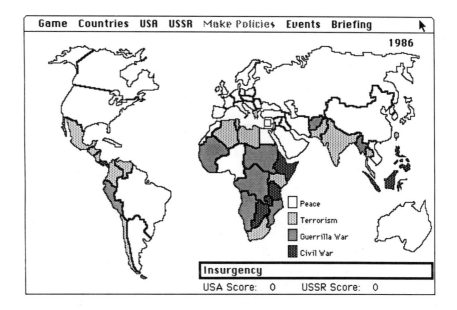

This display shows quite a bit of turbulence in the world. I take careful note of all the civil wars. Those in the Philippines, Indonesia, and Panama threaten friendly governments and must be stopped. Those in Zimbabwe and Tanzania affect neutral countries and are avenues of small opportunity. I decide to begin by examining the situation in the Philippines. The Closeup of the Philippines contains a surprise, as shown on the following page.

```
 Game  Countries  USA  USSR  Make Policies  Events  Briefing      ▸
┌──────────────────────── Closeup: Philippines ────────────────────────┐
                        USA Value              USSR Value
Relationship:           warm                   cool
Prestige Value:         27                     -13              { 44}
Military Aid:           $100 million           {$0 million}
Insurgency Aid:         $0 million          ↑ {$20 million}
Intervene--govt:        0 men                  {0 men}
Intervene--rebels:      0 men                  0 men
Economic Aid:           $400 million           $0 million
Destabilization:        No activity         ↑ Help dissidents
Pressure:               none                   none
Treaty:                 Conventional defense   No relations
Finlandization?         Invulnerable           Invulnerable
Annual Change:          tiny decrease          tiny decrease
               Values in {brackets} are maximum possible
Insurgency: civil war -- insurgency growing
Govt Philosophy:   right
Military Power:  Weak
Sphere of Influence:   Fairly USA
Govt Stability:   fair -- weakening slowly
Capital: Manila                  Insurgency: New People's Army
```

This display definitely calls for action. First is the notation of the civil war, and apparently the insurgents are growing stronger. It appears they will soon win unless something is done. The fact that this is a right-wing government with warm relations with the USA and cool relations toward the USSR means that I do *not* want this government to fall, especially because the Philippines are worth up to 44 points of prestige (the value in brackets on the right side of the display). If I can help the government out, my 27-point prestige score in the Philippines will grow, and if the government falls, I will surely lose those 27 points of prestige. Moreover, I have a conventional defense treaty with the government—only a nuclear defense treaty is more binding. It is obviously imperative that I save this regime. Fortunately, I have almost a free hand in the Philippines. The country's Sphere of

Influence value is "Fairly USA"—that's very good. Moreover, my conventional defense treaty establishes a strong diplomatic position for me, especially when compared with the USSR's lack of any treaty relationship. Plus, my diplomatic relationship with the Philippines is much stronger than the Soviets'. All the cards are in my hands.

Even better, the Soviets have foolishly attempted to both assist the insurgents, and destabilize the government as well. This tells me something very important: My Soviet adversaries are particularly belligerent this game—why else would they attempt such strong moves where the advantage is mine? I shall be in for a rough game. However, this can be turned to my advantage. As in judo, you can use your opponent's momentum against him—and I am about to do just that. I shall use the Soviets' belligerence to lay them low. They cannot possibly stand up to me over the Philippines. So I shall first challenge the Soviet Union here over their aid to the New People's Army.

CHALLENGING SOVIET ACTIONS

I bring up the USSR Actions window from the *Events* menu and flip through the pages until I find the relevant entry, which is shown on the next page.

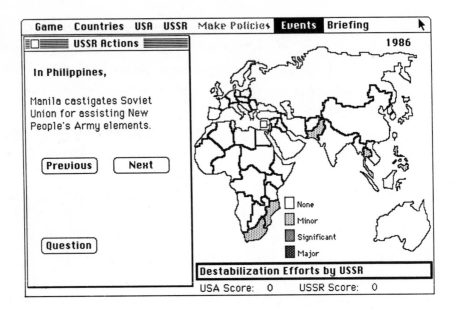

I press the *Question* button. The response comes back quickly:

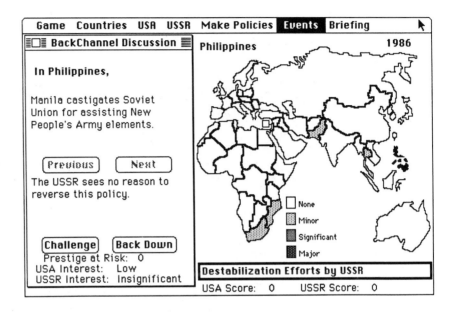

Apparently, the Soviets mean to test my mettle. However, I note several items here. First, my advisors seem to think that my own interest in this affair is low, while the Soviet interest is insignificant. I think that my interest in the matter is considerably higher than that, and I also know that one cannot trust one's advisors in the Expert-level game, but it is always nice to have a second opinion when you are playing Russian roulette with thermonuclear weapons. At least my advisors agree that American interest in the matter is greater than Soviet interest. I have the advantage.

The second thing I note is the wording of the Soviet reply. The USSR "sees no reason to reverse this policy." This is a reasonable wording. There is no bombast in it, no reference to military power, and no absolute refusal, either. It suggests that, if we merely point out a good reason to reverse the policy, they might do so. I therefore decide to challenge the Soviets publicly. Their response is:

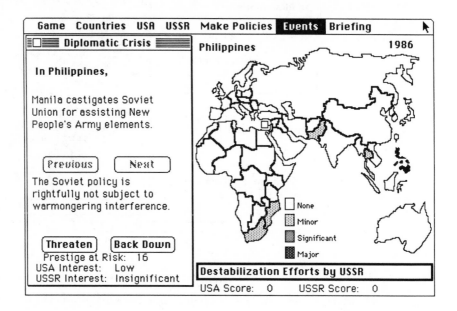

There are two items to note here: First is the prestige at stake. If I back down now, I shall lose 16 points of prestige. That would not be a good way to start the game. More important is the tone of the Soviet response. Even though they rejected my challenge, their wording is almost conciliatory. They say that their policy is "rightfully not subject" to my challenge. Their appeal to moral rights seems to be almost an excuse. Again, there is no sabre-rattling, no declaration of firmness, no absolutes. I decide to press my case to the next level:

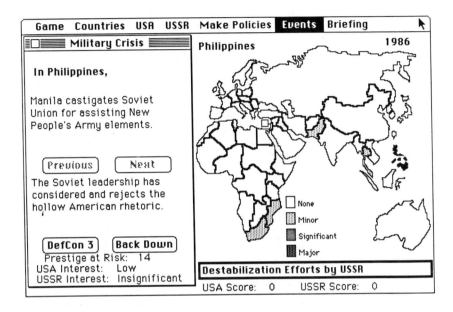

This surprises me in two ways. I had expected them to back down this time. Instead, they are standing firm. Was I wrong to escalate? Now I am in a tight spot. We are in a military crisis already. The Soviets are at DefCon 4, not a very dangerous level, but if I escalate, I will go to DefCon 3, and that runs a small risk of an accidental nuclear war. Moreover, if the Soviets continue to stand firm, they will go to DefCon 2, at which the risk of an accidental war is larger.

The other surprise is the amount of prestige at risk: At 14 points, it is actually lower than it was before. This is because the calculation of prestige at risk is deliberately but slightly randomized, just enough to rob the player of certainty.

I turn to the wording of the Soviet reply; again, it seems to be less than an absolute rejection: "The Soviet leadership has considered and rejects" my challenge. The fact that they took the time to think it over means that they are not sure of themselves. They are probably arguing among themselves even now. They are very close to caving in, if I can just push them a little harder. The problem is, I have very little maneuvering room left. I am already risking an accidental nuclear war, and if I escalate one more time, I will have lost all maneuvering room.

After much consideration, I decide to go ahead. I go to DefCon 3 and the Soviets back down:

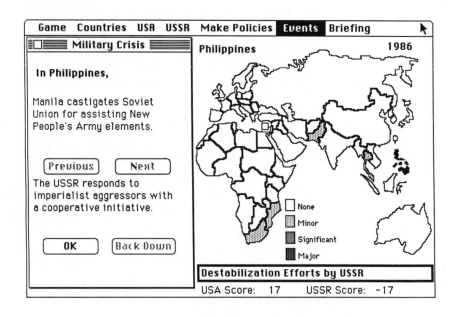

I stared them down! The success only gained me 17 points of prestige, and it greatly bothers me that I went all the way to DefCon 3 to get my victory, but I could not allow them to bring down the Philippine government. If I had backed down there, where in the world would I have been able to stand up to the Soviets? This was a scary crisis, too close for comfort, but it had to be done. As a reward, I have earned 17 points of prestige. I pat myself on the back.

I know that I have other work to attend to, but I decide it can wait while I check out what other actions the Soviets have been up to. I flip to the next Soviet action: an attempt to destabilize the government of Pakistan. I consult the Closeup for Pakistan:

```
 Game  Countries  USA  USSR  Make Policies  Events  Briefing        ▶
▢▤▤▤▤▤▤▤▤▤▤▤▤▤▤▤▤ Closeup: Pakistan ▤▤▤▤▤▤▤▤▤▤▤▤▤▤▤▤
                      USA Value              USSR Value
Relationship:         friendly              cool
Prestige Value:       23                    -18           { 60}
Military Aid:         $400 million          {$0 million}
Insurgency Aid:       $0 million            $0 million
Intervene--govt:      0 men                 {0 men}
Intervene--rebels:    0 men                 0 men
Economic Aid:         $400 million          $0 million
Destabilization:      No activity         ↑ Help dissidents
Pressure:             none                  none
Treaty:               {Military bases}      {Diplomatic relations}
Finlandization?       Invulnerable          Invulnerable
Annual Change:        tiny decrease         tiny decrease
                 Values in {brackets} are maximum possible
Insurgency:  minor terrorism -- insurgency growing
Govt Philosophy:   extreme right
Military Power:    Minor
Sphere of Influence:   Fairly USA
Govt Stability:    stable -- weakening slowly
Capital: Islamabad            Insurgency: Pushtun
```

Here is a right-wing government, friendly to the USA and cool to the USSR, and somewhat within my sphere of influence. I have a military-bases treaty with Pakistan, but the Soviets have diplomatic relations. The situation here is not as clear-cut as it was in the Philippines. Moreover, the Pakistani government is in no immediate danger of falling: the Closeup plainly says that the government is stable and weakening slowly; the Soviet attempts at destabilization will fail. Nevertheless, I decide to challenge them, promising myself that I will not pursue the matter into a military crisis. This time, the Soviets back down on the second step of the crisis, and I earn 4 more prestige points:

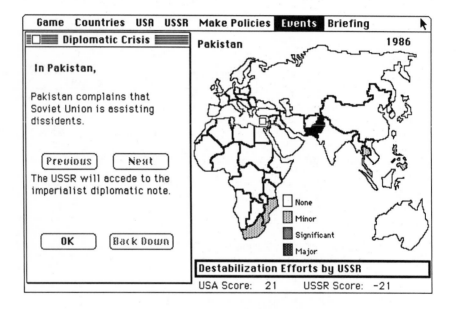

Now I seem to have established some diplomatic momentum in my favor. I continue looking through the news for items of interest. I come upon an item about Soviet attempts to destabilize Thailand; I happen to recall that Thailand is a US ally. This needs my attention; I check the Closeup for Thailand:

```
 Game  Countries  USA  USSR  Make Policies  Events  Briefing        ▶
▗▖▗▖▗▖▗▖▗▖▗▖▗▖▗▖▗▖▗▖▗▖ Closeup: Thailand ▗▖▗▖▗▖▗▖▗▖▗▖▗▖▗▖
                        USA Value              USSR Value
 Relationship:          warm                   cool
 Prestige Value:        31                     -17              { 57}
 Military Aid:          $400 million           {$0 million}
 Insurgency Aid:        $0 million             $0 million
 Intervene--govt:       {5,000 men}            {0 men}
 Intervene--rebels:     0 men                  0 men
 Economic Aid:          $400 million           $0 million
 Destabilization:       No activity          ↑ Help dissidents
 Pressure:              none                   none
 Treaty:                {Military bases}       {Diplomatic relations}
 Finlandization?        Invulnerable           Invulnerable
 Annual Change:         tiny decrease          tiny decrease
                  Values in {brackets} are maximum possible
 Insurgency:  minor terrorism -- insurgency growing
 Govt Philosophy:    extreme right
 Military Power:   Minor
 Sphere of Influence:    Slightly USA
 Govt Stability:   very strong -- weakening slowly
 Capital: Bangkok            Insurgency: insurgents
```

The situation seems to be in my favor. Thailand has warm relations with the USA and cool relations with the USSR. My treaty relations with Thailand are strong, and the country is slightly within my sphere of influence. This situation is less auspicious than that in Pakistan, but I still have the upper hand. I am beginning to believe that the Soviet intransigence in the Philippines was only to test my mettle, and now that I have demonstrated my forcefulness, they will be more reasonable. I decide to press my case and challenge the Soviets. The crisis reaches DefCon 3 before the Soviets back down. I pressed my luck again, but now my score is up to 56, and I have really cowed the Soviets.

Continuing in the Soviet actions folder, I go on the diplomatic warpath. I find a whole series of Soviet attempts to sign various treaties with American clients—countries such as Colombia, Saudi Arabia, Egypt, Israel, Morocco, Honduras, and Venezuela. I challenge each action, and the Soviets back down on each one after registering a small protest. I earn a few points on each one. When the dust has settled, I have raised my score to 74 points. This is really the best way to earn points in *Balance of Power.* You do not risk starting a war if you never enter a military crisis, and you can just keep on racking up the points, a few at a time.

A few minor crises suffice to drive Soviet weapons out of Chile and Honduras; they were easy victories because the United States has such a solid sphere of influence in Latin America. Then I press my luck again: I challenge Soviet economic aid to Nicaragua. This is risky business. Nicaragua is ambiguous territory. While it is historically very much in the American sphere, the last seven years of Marxist rule have given the Soviets a claim to that country. I press all the way to DefCon 3, and the Soviets back down. That was a dangerous move. Nicaragua is simply not worth risking nuclear war over. Twice before I have gone this far, but those cases were matters of greater importance. I resolve to be more careful.

The very next news item gives me an opportunity to test my resolve. The Soviets are sending weapons to the Anya-Nya insurgents in the Sudan. I bring up the Closeup for Sudan:

```
┌─────────────────────────────────────────────────────────────────────┐
│  Game  Countries  USA  USSR  Make Policies  Events  Briefing       ▶ │
├─────────────────────────────────────────────────────────────────────┤
│ ▤□▬▬▬▬▬▬▬▬▬▬▬▬▬▬▬▬▬▬ Closeup: Sudan ▬▬▬▬▬▬▬▬▬▬▬▬▬▬▬▬▬              │
│                      USA Value            USSR Value                 │
│ Relationship:        cordial              cool                       │
│ Prestige Value:      1                    -2              { 10}       │
│ Military Aid:        $0 million           $0 million                 │
│ Insurgency Aid:      $0 million         ↑ $20 million                │
│ Intervene--govt:     {0 men}             {0 men}                     │
│ Intervene--rebels:   0 men                0 men                      │
│ Economic Aid:        $400 million         $0 million                 │
│ Destabilization:     No activity          No activity                │
│ Pressure:            none                 none                       │
│ Treaty:              {Trade relations}    No relations               │
│ Finlandization?      Invulnerable         Invulnerable               │
│ Annual Change:       tiny decrease        tiny decrease              │
│             Values in {brackets} are maximum possible               │
│ Insurgency:  major guerrilla war -- insurgency growing              │
│ Govt Philosophy:   slight right                                      │
│ Military Power:    Insignificant                                     │
│ Sphere of Influence:   Slightly USSR                                 │
│ Govt Stability:   very strong -- weakening slowly                   │
│ Capital: Khartoum          Insurgency: Anya-Nya                     │
└─────────────────────────────────────────────────────────────────────┘
```

This is not a reassuring situation. The Sudanese government has cordial relations with the USA, but look at the prestige values: 1 point for the USA, −2 points for the USSR, with a maximum possible value of only 10 points. Here is a country that is not worth fighting for. Moreover, my diplomatic position there is weak: Although I have a trade-relations treaty with Sudan, the area is slightly within the Soviet sphere of influence. This is an ambiguous situation, the likes of which often cause wars. I decide to shy away from a confrontation with the Soviets over Sudan.

Afterthought: This was probably a mistake. While Sudan is indeed slightly within the Soviet sphere of influence, I need not have given up so easily. I could have started to develop a relationship by first sending a little bit of economic aid, then a small amount of military aid in later turns. These friendly gestures, being fairly innocuous, might well have gotten past a Soviet challenge. They would have warmed Sudanese-American relations and made possible an improved treaty relationship, which would have provided the basis for standing firm against further Soviet challenges. Spheres of influence are important, but so are treaty relationships. This general tactic of gradually increasing aid, which I call *developing a relationship,* is an important way to break another superpower's grip on a nation.

Next, I discover that Mozambique is the object of a great deal of Soviet activity:

```
┌────────────────────────────────────────────────────────────────────────┐
│  Game  Countries  USA  USSR  Make Policies  Events  Briefing        ▶  │
├────────────────────────────────────────────────────────────────────────┤
│ ▤□▤▤▤▤▤▤▤▤▤▤▤▤▤▤▤▤▤▤▤ Closeup: Mozambique ▤▤▤▤▤▤▤▤▤▤▤▤▤▤▤▤▤▤▤▤▤      │
│                      USA Value           USSR Value                      │
│ Relationship:        cordial             hostile                        │
│ Prestige Value:      0                   -2              { 3}           │
│ Military Aid:        $0 million          {$0 million}                   │
│ Insurgency Aid:      $0 million        ↑ {$20 million}                  │
│ Intervene--govt:     {0 men}             {0 men}                        │
│ Intervene--rebels:   0 men             ↑ {5,000 men}                    │
│ Economic Aid:        $0 million          {$0 million}                   │
│ Destabilization:     No activity       ↑ Help dissidents               │
│ Pressure:            none                none                           │
│ Treaty:              No relations        {No relations}                 │
│ Finlandization?      Invulnerable        Very High                      │
│ Annual Change:       tiny decrease       tiny decrease                  │
│               Values in {brackets} are maximum possible                 │
│ Insurgency:  minor guerrilla war -- insurgency growing                  │
│ Govt Philosophy:   very right                                           │
│ Military Power:    Insignificant                                        │
│ Sphere of Influence:   Strongly USSR                                    │
│ Govt Stability:    very strong -- weakening slowly                      │
│ Capital: Maputo            Insurgency: Makonde                          │
└────────────────────────────────────────────────────────────────────────┘
```

Here is a right-wing government that is strongly anti-communist, and the Soviets are doing everything in their power to overthrow that regime. They are sending weapons to the insurgents, they are destabilizing the government, and, most outrageous of all, they have sent 5,000 troops to help the guerrillas. I would very much like to help the government, but three things stop me. First, the country is strongly within the Soviet sphere of influence. Second, I have no treaty relationship to justify any interference. Third, Mozambique is worth, at most, only 3 prestige points. It is just not worth a confrontation. Let them have it.

The other country that is attracting some Soviet attention is Indonesia:

Game Countries USA USSR Make Policies Events Briefing		▶
Closeup: Indonesia		
	USA Value	**USSR Value**
Relationship:	cordial	cool
Prestige Value:	16	-22 { 72}
Military Aid:	$20 million	{$0 million}
Insurgency Aid:	$0 million	↑ {$20 million}
Intervene--govt:	{0 men}	{0 men}
Intervene--rebels:	0 men	0 men
Economic Aid:	$0 million	$0 million
Destabilization:	No activity	No activity
Pressure:	none	none
Treaty:	Trade relations	No relations
Finlandization?	Invulnerable	Invulnerable
Annual Change:	tiny decrease	tiny decrease
Values in {brackets} are maximum possible		
Insurgency: civil war -- insurgency growing		
Govt Philosophy: very right		
Military Power: Minor		
Sphere of Influence: Slightly USSR		
Govt Stability: very strong -- weakening slowly		
Capital: Jakarta	**Insurgency:** Communist Party	

Here is an important country, important because it's worth up to 72 points of prestige. Moreover, I have cordial relations with Indonesia, while its relations with the USSR are cool. I also have a trade-relations treaty, while the Soviets have none. On the other hand, Indonesia is slightly within the Soviet sphere of influence. This is not a solid situation for me, and I decide not to challenge the Soviet actions. Instead, later in the turn when I make my own policies, I'll send some aid of my own to help the government.

There are, of course, many other Soviet actions not mentioned here. I ignore almost all Soviet actions in Eastern bloc nations. If the Soviets want to send troops into East Germany, let them. There's no point in picking a fight you can't win.

I have gone through all the Soviet actions and challenged all those that I wanted to challenge. Before I proceed to the next part of my move, I wish to explain a crucial aspect of my strategy. I made sure to challenge the Soviets first in the area in which I felt strongest: the Philippines. I could be certain of victory here, and that victory created momentum which I then used in Pakistan, where my position was weaker. That victory paved the way for the next victory, and so on. The trick here is to start where you are strongest, and the Philippines are always a bastion of American diplomatic strength. The other side of this coin is to avoid losing any crises. Winning a crisis increases your *Pugnacity* value, while losing a crisis decreases it. *Pugnacity* affects *Adventurousness*, which in turn determines the willingness of the computer to stand up to you in a crisis. In other words, every time you win a crisis, you make it easier to win the next crisis. Every time you lose a crisis, you make it that much harder to win the next crisis.

MAKING POLICY

I am now ready to begin making my own policies. There are two tasks here: to determine what action is needed, and decide whether or not I can get away with the action. Making a policy that the Soviets can force me to rescind is bad business, so I must guess beforehand whether or not my contemplated action can withstand a Soviet challenge.

I check the maps for insurgency, coups, and Finlandization, noting any countries that are dark gray or gray. These are the ones that most need attention.

The very first item of business is to save the Philippine government. I may have been able to chase out the Soviets, but there is still the native insurgency. I feel confident of my position in the Philippines, so I send large amounts of military aid, backed up by a direct intervention with 100,000 American troops. That's a pretty hefty intervention, but I want to finish off the civil war quickly and then pull out the troops. Besides, the Soviets won't challenge me after being so decisively beaten in the crisis over their aid to the rebels.

Indonesia gets $100 million in military aid. I'd like to send more, but I feel weak here. The Soviets will probably challenge me, but maybe I'll get lucky and sneak it by.

Panama is another country caught in a civil war. Feeling secure in my own back yard, I send $100 million in military aid and 5,000 troops. This isn't much, but Panama is a small country and this force should be more than adequate to defeat the insurgents.

The Coups display shows that South Africa is facing the chance of a coup d'etat, so I send $1 billion in economic aid. I am not optimistic, but perhaps things will improve.

On the offensive side, I send $100 million in aid to the Contras in Nicaragua. This should keep the Sandinistas busy for awhile. I am satisfied with my actions for the turn and select "Next Turn" from the *Game* menu.

THE SOVIET RESPONSES

The Soviets immediately challenge my intervention in the Philippines. I am surprised by this; perhaps a smaller intervention would not have earned their ire. Now I definitely have a problem. If I back down on this intervention, the communist New People's Army will probably win the civil war. I will lose the friendship of the Philippine government and considerable integrity to boot. This is a very serious challenge; I cannot afford to back down. I stand firm as the crisis escalates up to DefCon 4; the Soviets balk at the prospect of going to DefCon 3 and back down:

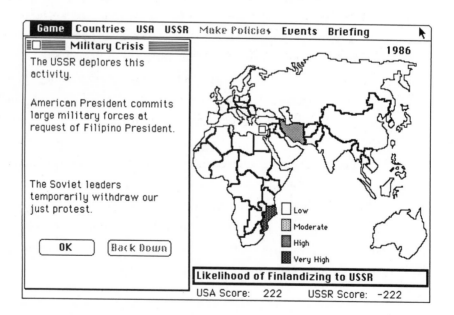

This is a major victory, for my score shoots up to 222 points. In a single crisis, I have earned more than 120 points! "That's the game," I smile to myself. "He will never be able to recover from this catastrophe."

However, the Soviets then challenge me on my military aid to Indonesia. The crisis escalates to DefCon 4:

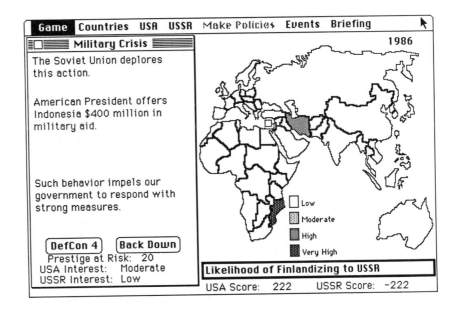

I decide to back down at this point. My diplomatic position was not strong to start with, and the Soviet message is strongly worded: "Such behavior impels our government to respond with strong measures." This is not the limp-wristed wording they used earlier which plaintively wrung its hands over issues of rights. This is an unblinking threat of military force ("strong measures"). These guys aren't bluffing this time. I back down and eat the 20-point loss. I can afford it; I am still way ahead.

The Soviets follow up with another challenge, this time for my economic aid to South Africa:

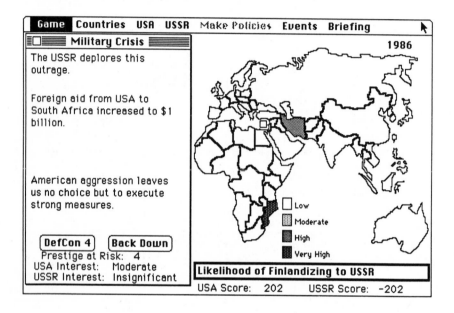

Again we have that stern phrase "strong measures." My advisors seem to feel that my interest in the policy is moderate, while the Soviet interest is insignificant; if I were taking their advice I would stand firm, but the decisive factor in my mind is the amount of prestige at risk. With only 4 points at stake, I am unwilling to risk an accidental nuclear war. Besides, I don't think that the South African government is in that much trouble. I back down.

The Soviets continue their offensive by challenging

me on my troop intervention in Panama, but I stand firm and they quickly back off. Another challenge over my aid to the Nicaraguan Contras produces an equally rapid American retreat. On one last throw of the dice, the Soviets attempt to scare me out of my military aid to Panama, but I stared them down earlier over the troops and I stare them down again.

CONCLUSIONS ON TURN 1

It has been a very successful turn. I have stood up to the Soviets on several crucial issues and defended my clients in the Philippines, Pakistan, Panama, and Thailand. I have foiled their support for Nicaragua (even though I had to back down on my own aid to the Contras) and forced them to repudiate a wide variety of treaty arrangements. The only unmitigated crisis losses I suffered were in Indonesia and South Africa. The situation in South Africa troubles me. Although the government there is not in immediate danger, my backing down will only encourage further Soviet action there. I may well be forced to make a stand on South Africa later. If so, backing down now was not an auspicious beginning.

Except for that one cloud on the horizon, Turn 1 was highly successful. On to Turn 2!

*T*URN 2: *1987*

The Major Events display for Turn 2 has several surprises for me:

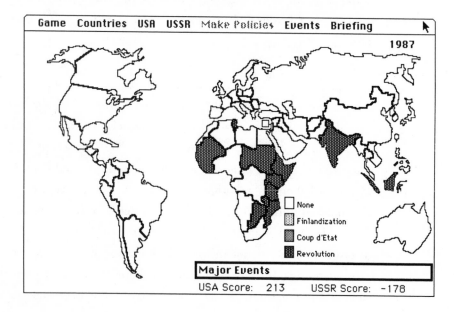

The first surprise is the large number of revolutions that took place in a single year. Ten countries, most in Africa, underwent revolutions. Most are minor countries that will not affect the balance of power, but the loss of Indonesia definitely hurt. Much more surprising was the revolution in India. On the last turn, India was only in a state of terrorism, and that exploded into a civil war within a single year. That definitely surprised me. I examine the Closeup for India:

266

```
 Game  Countries  USA  USSR  Make Policies  Events  Briefing        ▶
▣▣▢════════════════ Closeup: India ═══════════════════════
                        USA Value           USSR Value
Relationship:          cordial             cold
Prestige Value:        6                   -22              { 49}
Military Aid:          $0 million          {$0 million}
Insurgency Aid:        $0 million        ↑ {$20 million}
Intervene--govt:       {0 men}             {0 men}
Intervene--rebels:     0 men               0 men
Economic Aid:        ↓ $0 million          {$0 million}
Destabilization:       No activity       ↑ Fund opposition
Pressure:              none                none
Treaty:                {No relations}      {No relations}
Finlandization?        Invulnerable        Invulnerable
Annual Change:         tiny decrease       small increase
                 Values in {brackets} are maximum possible
Insurgency:  rampant terrorism -- insurgency growing
Govt Philosophy:   right
Military Power:   Weak
Sphere of Influence:    Fairly USSR
Govt Stability:   very strong -- weakening slowly
Capital: New Delhi          Insurgency: Sikh movement
```

This situation calls out for quick American action. Here is a pro-American regime that is facing a developing insurgency. To make matters worse, the Soviets are helping the insurgents and attempting to destabilize the government. I resolve to assist the new government, but I'm nervous about the Soviet sphere of influence here. I opt for the lowest levels of military and economic aid in the hope of getting a foot in the door. If these survive a Soviet challenge, I can increase them next year.

SOVIET ACTIONS

Next, check out Soviet activities for the year. The very first item in the folder is a real bombshell: The Soviets have invaded Iran with 100,000 men! Apparently my sabre-rattling behavior in the past crises has

weakened their inhibitions, and they are now playing hardball. I immediately check the Closeup for Iran. The situation is quite hopeless:

Game Countries USA USSR Make Policies Events Briefing		
Closeup: Iran		
	USA Value	**USSR Value**
Relationship:	cold	cool
Prestige Value:	-112	-49 { 205}
Military Aid:	{$0 million}	$0 million
Insurgency Aid:	{$20 million}	{$0 million}
Intervene--govt:	{0 men}	{0 men}
Intervene--rebels:	0 men	↑ 100,000 men
Economic Aid:	{$0 million}	$0 million
Destabilization:	No activity	No activity
Pressure:	none	none
Treaty:	{No relations}	{Diplomatic relations}
Finlandization?	Invulnerable	Moderate
Annual Change:	tiny increase	moderate decrease
Values in {brackets} are maximum possible		
Insurgency: slight unrest -- insurgency weakening		
Govt Philosophy: extreme right		
Military Power: Moderate		
Sphere of Influence: Slightly USSR		
Govt Stability: very strong -- weakening fast		
Capital: Teheran	**Insurgency:** Tudeh	

The Iranian government hates America more than
it hates the Soviets (that will change quickly enough). I have no diplomatic relations or policy commitments to back up any claims for helping the Iranians. In fact, I am giving $20 million to help the insurgents.
In other words, the Soviets and the Americans are on the same side!
How can I possibly convince the Soviets that I am seriously opposed to
their invasion? I have no credible basis for opposing the Soviet invasion. I must give up Iran to the Soviets. This hurts: Iran is worth 205
prestige points. I have suffered a major loss here.

I move on to the next item, which is even more

explosive: The Soviets have invaded South Korea! This time I don't even bother to check the Closeup. The United States has a long history of close relations with South Korea. We have a conventional defense treaty with the South Korean government. We went to war once before to defend that country and I have absolutely no reservations about doing so again. I will take this crisis as far as I need to go. Fortunately, the Soviets back down immediately.

Now follows a series of minor crises in which the Soviets back down without resisting my challenges. They quickly back down from their attempt to destabilize Pakistan. In a surprise move, they accept my challenge to their destabilization of South Africa. Perhaps I was wrong to cave in over South Africa last turn. I shall be more assertive on this subject in the future. The real bonus is my gain in prestige from this crisis: My score leaps from some 220 points to 371 points—a 150-point gain from a single crisis! Apparently my previous retreat over South Africa had created the impression that the country was within the Soviet sphere, which impression made the Soviet retreat this time seem all the more stunning. In any event, I have a taken a huge lead now.

The Soviets also back down from attempts to destabilize Chile, Turkey, the Philippines, Greece, and Mexico. However, they send troops to invade Zimbabwe, Tunisia, and Tanzania; I choose to let these outrages pass. I have the lead; why risk everything over issues that are probably worth only a few points?

I now examine the Insurgency map. My interventions in the Philippines and Panama seem to have turned the situation around quite satisfactorily. I could pull the troops out, but I will leave them in until they are needed elsewhere. Since there are no civil wars, I have little need for drastic action. I note a small guerrilla war in Peru. As a precautionary measure, I send some military aid to Peru; this should keep its developing insurgency under control.

The Coups map also shows a more stable world. The only regime ripe for a coup is in Ethiopia; after considering the Closeup of that country, I decide to take a hands-off approach:

```
 Game  Countries  USA  USSR  Make Policies  Events  Briefing        ▶

▭▬▬▬▬▬▬▬▬▬▬▬▬▬▬▬▬ Closeup: Ethiopia ▬▬▬▬▬▬▬▬▬▬▬▬
                          USA Value              USSR Value
Relationship:             warm                   enemy
Prestige Value:            26                     -38           { 40}
Military Aid:          ↑ $20 million          ↓ {$0 million}
Insurgency Aid:       ↓ $0 million           ↑ {$20 million}
Intervene--govt:         {0 men}             ↓ {0 men}
Intervene--rebels:        0 men                  0 men
Economic Aid:         ↓ $0 million             {$0 million}
Destabilization:          No activity         ↑ {Support coup d'etat}
Pressure:                 none                   none
Treaty:                   No relations           {No relations}
Finlandization?           Invulnerable           Invulnerable
Annual Change:            tiny decrease          small increase
                   Values in {brackets} are maximum possible
Insurgency: rampant terrorism -- insurgency weakening
Govt Philosophy:    very right
Military Power:     Weak
Sphere of Influence:    Very strongly USSR
Govt Stability:    very shaky -- weakening fast
Capital: Addis Ababa          Insurgency: Eritrean LF
```

The Soviet grip on Ethiopia is too strong. This country is very strongly within the Soviet sphere of influence. It's a shame; I am now getting 26 points of prestige from Ethiopia and the Soviets are losing 38 points. I would very much like to freeze the situation right there, but there seems to be little that I can do to influence events without causing a confrontation with the Soviets. Too bad.

The Philippines seem to be vulnerable to a coup, so I send massive economic aid. Economic performance is the determining factor in the initiation of a coup d'etat. Otherwise, the world seems quiet. The Finlandization maps show nothing of interest, so I decide to move on to Turn 3.

TURN 2: THE SOVIET RESPONSES, AND CONCLUSIONS

The Soviets challenge me on only two issues: my military and economic aid to India. I back down on both issues. I am not going to throw away my big lead over tactical concerns.

This was a quiet turn. It started off with a bang, but there were no great crises. The two sides seem to be getting each other's measure. I have come to accept Soviet hegemony in much of Africa (except for Egypt, Morocco, and South Africa). The USSR now seems to accept my freedom of action in the Philippines and South Africa. Except for the numerous Soviet invasions in Africa and Iran, the world seems to be settling down. That's good—I have a lead so commanding that the only way I can fail now is to get into a war, so my primary goal for the future will be avoiding major confrontations with my Soviet adversaries.

TURN 3: 1988

The third turn begins with my score jumping up by another 50 points, to 380, while the Soviet score is −323. I am a little surprised by this development, for the Major Events map for this year reveals only some acts of Finlandization and another revolution in India. I investigate the Minor Country News to determine what's going on. The acts of Finlandization were numerous; it appears that the Soviet invasions and the crises between the two superpowers have frightened many world leaders, and they are hurrying to patch up their differences with unfriendly superpowers. Thus, Cuba and Indonesia both Finlandize to me, while Afghanistan draws itself deeper into the Soviet embrace. A host of minor countries—Kenya, Tanzania, Zimbabwe, and Mexico—Finlandize to me, boosting my score even further. You throw your weight around and you get results.

A check of the Insurgency map shows that the Soviet invasions in Africa have triggered a wave of political violence:

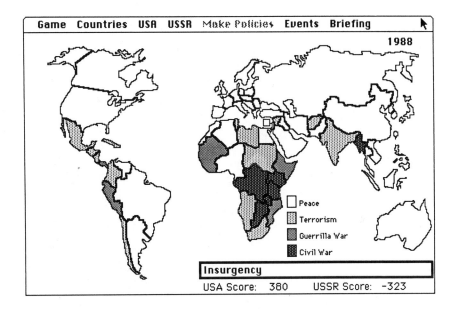

It would seem that Soviet aggression has not created a new Soviet bloc in central Africa but a gigantic Red Vietnam. Perhaps my reluctance to get involved was lucky. The surprise is Iran. Although the USSR sent 100,000 troops to help the insurgents, the government there seems to have matters well in hand.

The Coups map shows that Turkey, Pakistan, and South Africa are all in some danger of a coup, so I send massive amounts of economic aid to the first two countries. I send less to South Africa because I am not sure that I can withstand a Soviet challenge there. To get all this money, I suspend economic aid to Egypt and Israel, neither of which really needs the money.

On the next page, the Finlandization charts show a world made nervous by superpower adventurism.

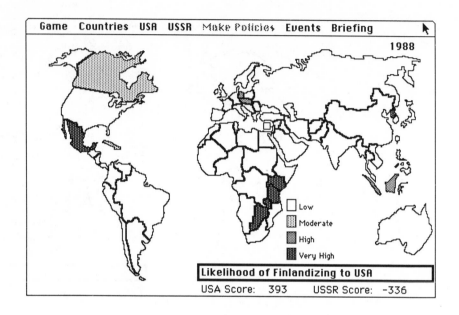

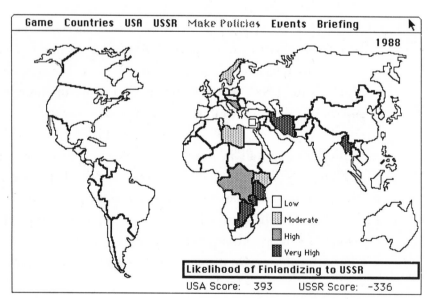

Still, I dare not take action on any of these issues. The Soviets would not stand still for my applying diplomatic pressure to any of their clients.

I check the Soviet actions for Turn 3. Only four trigger crises. A Soviet attempt to destabilize South Africa draws a quick American response and an equally quick retraction. I also shut down their attempts to provide economic and military aid to Nicaragua, gaining a dozen points in the process without having to take matters into a military crisis. I also jump on them for providing weapons to insurgents in Panama, which they immediately withdraw. Otherwise, I let them run riot in Africa and the Eastern bloc. Their actions don't seem to be doing them much good.

The only other policy action I carry out is some military aid to Sweden, which has been showing signs of possible Finlandization to the Soviet Union. Some additional weapons should bolster their confidence.

TURN 3: SOVIET RESPONSES, AND CONCLUSIONS

The Kremlin challenges me on just one issue: my economic aid to South Africa. I stand firm and they eventually back down, losing some 30 points in the process. I have established that South Africa is undeniably within the American sphere.

This turn was even more quiet than the previous one, a development that suits me just fine. With my lead, the last thing I want now are tough situations that force me to choose between losing a good friend (and lots of points) and risking a nuclear war. So far, my restraint with the Soviets seems to be doing just that.

*T*URN 4: *1989*

There was a tremendous amount of activity this turn:

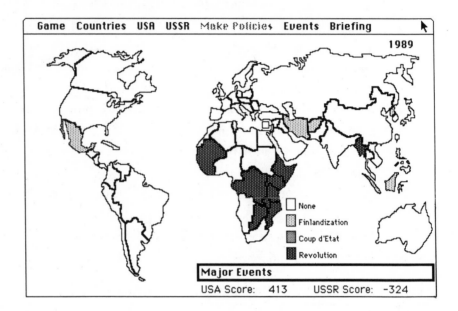

The two most noteworthy events were acts of Finlandization. Iran finally broke down and Finlandized to the USSR, giving them 51 points, while North Korea Finlandized to me, yielding 47 points for me. Thus, the two actions just about canceled each other out. Apparently my own belligerence in crises with the Soviets has made an impression on the North Koreans, who are hedging their bets and building a stronger relationship with the USA even while they remain firmly in the Soviet camp.

The various revolutions in Africa almost all worked against the Soviets and in my favor, except for the revolution in Ethiopia, which threw out a pro-American government. It appears that the Kremlin has mired itself in a real mess in central Africa from which it may never extricate itself. A lengthy investigation reveals the source of their troubles. As soon as their side wins the civil war, the Soviet troops depart. But the African countries, brutalized by so much civil war, do not find domestic peace so easily; as soon as the troops depart, civil war flares up again. The Soviets are forced to send the troops back. If they could afford to just leave the troops in one place for awhile, they could bring stability to their African clients, but they have so many troops tied down all over the world that they cannot afford to leave them in one place; they must instead shuttle them from one danger zone to another. The Soviets have overextended themselves and are paying the price.

In other matters, India is caught in another civil war; I try to take advantage of this opportunity and slip in a little aid to the insurgents. Mexico, Peru, and South Africa continue to have economic problems, so I ship them all increased economic aid. The Finlandization situation now looks fairly quiet.

Only three Soviet actions earn my attention: yet another attempt to destabilize South Africa, and more attempts to get military and economic aid to Nicaragua. The Kremlin backs down from all three without so much as a whimper of protest.

I decide that the time has come to eliminate the communist government of Nicaragua. I have established my sphere of influence, so I send $100 million in weapons to the Contras. We shall see if the USSR tries to stop me.

TURN 4: SOVIET RESPONSES, AND CONCLUSIONS

The Soviets challenged me on my insurgency aid to India; I stood firm for one step, then decided that they were serious, so I backed down and lost 33 points. They also challenged my economic aid to South Africa, but they lost that crisis and 2 points. Significantly, they didn't raise a whisper about my weapons shipments to Nicaragua.

I am feeling pretty good about my situation right now. I have a huge lead; all I need do now is coast to the end of the game and victory. However, I have beaten them so roundly that I have half a mind to look for some opportunities. If I can find some safe areas for offensive action, I will take them.

*T*URN 5: 1990

The score at the outset of Turn 5 is 534 to −352; I am feeling quite pleased with myself. I am halfway through the game and have a gigantic lead. The Major Events display shows little of concern:

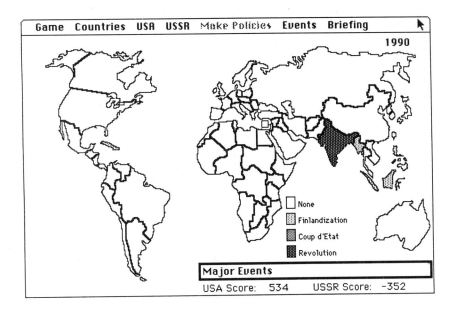

The revolution in India could only work in my favor. I decide that it would be worthwhile to attempt an opening in India. I shall begin with the most innocuous of actions, a treaty of diplomatic relations with the new government. Surely the Kremlin will not object to so unthreatening an action. Just to be sure, though, I consult the Closeup for India, which is shown on the next page.

```
 Game  Countries  USA  USSR  Make Policies  Events  Briefing        ▶
▕▤□▕▔▔▔▔▔▔▔▔▔▔▔▔▔▔▔▔ Closeup: India ▤▔▔▔▔▔▔▔▔▔▔▔▔▔▔▕
                    USA Value              USSR Value
Relationship:       warm                   enemy
Prestige Value:     26                     -44            { 49}
Military Aid:       $0 million           ↓ {$0 million}
Insurgency Aid:   ↓ {$0 million}           {$0 million}
Intervene--govt:    {0 men}                {0 men}
Intervene--rebels:  0 men                ↑ {5,000 men}
Economic Aid:       $0 million           ↓ {$0 million}
Destabilization:    No activity          ↑ {Support coup d'etat}
Pressure:           none                   none
Treaty:             No relations           {No relations}
Finlandization?     Very High              Very High
Annual Change:      huge increase          huge increase
                 Values in {brackets} are maximum possible
Insurgency:  slight unrest -- insurgency weakening
Govt Philosophy:    moderate right
Military Power:     Insignificant
Sphere of Influence:   Moderately USSR
Govt Stability:   very strong -- strengthening fast
Capital: New Delhi            Insurgency: Sikh movement
```

This is great! After all that interference, all that activity, the Soviets have managed to make themselves more hated than before, and simultaneously contributed to my improved position in India. (Just three turns ago, India provided me with 6 points of prestige and the Soviets with −22 points; now the values are 26 and −44.) This was achieved without my ever getting any aid into the country. Although much of the improvement in the situation is due to my many crisis victories, I believe that the Soviet meddling in Indian affairs has also played a role in the shift. My position in India is good. There is the matter of the moderate Soviet sphere of influence, but I think it is worthwhile to at least see what I can get away with. I go ahead with a diplomatic relations treaty with India:

280

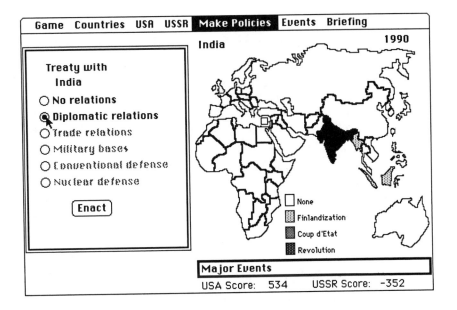

The Insurgency display shows little of interest. Peru is still struggling with its insurgency, so I increase military aid to that country. There are still quite a few guerrilla wars going in Africa; I'm glad I'm not caught up in that mess.

I decide that now is the time to make my move on Nicaragua. To establish a sound military position, I put 5,000 troops in Honduras. Then I send 5,000 soldiers to intervene in favor of the Contras. Let's see how the USSR reacts to *that*.

The Coups display indicates developing problems with many of my allies. I send massive economic aid to Mexico, Turkey, Peru, Chile, and South Africa. I hope I can keep these regimes afloat.

Now it is time to check the Soviet Union's latest activities. It seems like a rehash of old activities. They are still attempting to destabilize South Africa. A stern warning sends them packing. They make a brief resistance over their military and economic aid to Nicaragua before caving in and losing 11 points.

TURN FIVE: SOVIET RESPONSES, AND CONCLUSIONS

Here I make my first big mistake. The Soviets challenge my treaty with India and I decide to test their mettle. All of a sudden I am facing a 124-point loss if I back down, and furious Soviet rhetoric. This is the type of situation that loses games. I am sorely tempted to stand firm; after all, that's a lot of points to just throw away. Why not just stare the Russkis down and win big? It's hard to be cold and logical in a situation like this, but I know that I have to back down. It would be insanity to escalate in the hope that they will be intimidated. I don't know that they will back down; it could go either way. If I am right and win, it means only that I will win the game more gloriously than I otherwise would. If I am wrong and lose the crisis, then I will lose the entire game. It's just not worth the risk. I *must* back down, and eat the 124 points. Ouch! That's what I get for succumbing to adventurous impulses. I should have just left India alone.

The Soviets also challenge me on my economic aid to South Africa. Still smarting from the loss over India, there is no way I will back down here, and they quickly retreat.

Turn 5 would have been a good turn for me had I not failed so badly over India. I made two mistakes, and they were both of the same nature: I was probing to see what I could get away with. The first mistake was trying to get a diplomatic-relations treaty with India in the first place. That should not have been fatal; you can always back out of a weak policy when it is challenged. The second mistake was the fatal one; it was the cavalier decision to test the Kremlin's mettle once they had challenged me. I have done that before; the mistake this time was failing to realize that the cost of backing down would be so high this time. (The reason for the very high cost of backing down in this crisis will be explained later.) If I had given the same care to that decision that I gave to most of my regular decisions, I would not have gotten myself into that mess. *Balance of Power* is an unforgiving game; one slip and you suffer a big loss.

*T*URN 6: *1991*

Turn 6 started with more bad news. Although my own score recovered a little from the drubbing it took in the Indian crisis, the Soviets' score leapt to −103. In just a few moments the scores have gone from 545 and −365 to 444 and −103. My lead has shrunk from 910 points to 545 points. Ouch!

I try to determine where things went wrong. A check of the Minor Country News quickly shows the problem. Iran has again Finlandized to the Soviet Union, gaining it 51 points and costing me the same number of points. A revolution in Ethiopia finally ousted the pro-American government there, gaining another 54 points for the USSR. Other revolutions gained 25 more points for the Kremlin. In a single turn, they picked up 130 points. I begin to think that maybe my smug strategy of holding onto my gains was a mistake.

The various state-of-the-world displays show little action or opportunity for advancement. There are some minor guerrilla wars going on, but nothing that looks like a major opportunity. I see that I will have problems keeping Turkey and South Africa from undergoing coups. Otherwise, things are quiet.

The Soviets aren't up to anything odd either. The USSR Actions window reveals the usual list of shifting allocations of troops and weapons to the various Eastern bloc nations. Nothing that I want to involve myself in, except for still another attempt to send military aid to Nicaragua. These guys will never give up! Once again, I send them packing.

For my own actions, I decide to make a move on Indonesia. I had been intimidated out of giving aid to Indonesia at the beginning of the game, but nothing has happened there for some time, so I decide to try my luck. *This time*, though, I will be considerably more careful about backing down if I am challenged. My first step is to institute a diplomatic-relations treaty with Indonesia. We'll see how the Soviets react.

Otherwise, I send more military aid to Turkey in a desperate effort to help prop up the regime; I also send more economic aid to South Africa.

TURN 6: SOVIET RESPONSES, AND CONCLUSIONS

The Soviets did not challenge my new treaty with Indonesia; I may have the opening I wanted! In fact, they did not challenge anything.

I am now trying to recover the initiative in this game. I would desperately like to get a foot in the door somewhere. The Kremlin has effectively shut me out of most of the volatile regions of the world. I will try to further my position in Indonesia, but I wish that there were some way to exert influence in Iran, India, or Africa.

TURN 7: 1992

The beginning of Turn 7 heightens my fears that the Soviets are eating away at my lead. The score now stands at 493 to −68. My lead is now only 561 points. The Major Events display shows why:

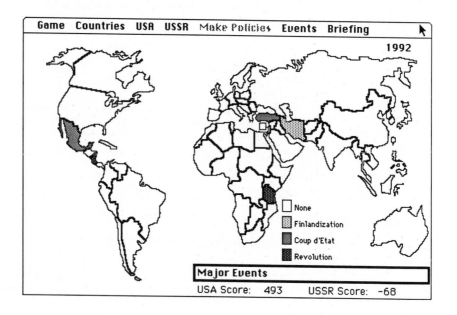

There were coups in Mexico and Turkey that could not have been beneficial to my score; Iran again Finlandized to the Soviet Union. The only bright note is the Contra victory in Nicaragua. Consultation with the Minor Country News shows that this gained me all of 9 points.

The Soviets have lost patience with the interminable war in Iran and send in a full 500,000 troops. The Iranians had

Finlandized to the Soviet Union numerous times, but the continuing Soviet intervention in Iran kept poisoning relations between the two countries. The enlarged Soviet intervention is outrageous, but I know that objecting would be futile. I must watch in silence as they simply conquer Iran. They are also very active in Africa, sending large amounts of weapons to their clients. Africa is turning into a gigantic battleground.

I decide to explore my opening in Indonesia more closely. The Closeup is interesting:

```
 Game  Countries  USA  USSR  Make Policies  Events  Briefing        ▶
▭                        Closeup: Indonesia
                      USA Value              USSR Value
Relationship:         close                  cold
Prestige Value:       55                     -34              { 72}
Military Aid:         $0 million             {$0 million}
Insurgency Aid:       {$0 million}           {$0 million}
Intervene--govt:      {0 men}                {0 men}
Intervene--rebels:    0 men                  0 men
Economic Aid:         $0 million             {$0 million}
Destabilization:      No activity            No activity
Pressure:             none                   none
Treaty:               Diplomatic relations   {Diplomatic relations}
Finlandization?       High                   Invulnerable
Annual Change:        small increase         tiny decrease
                   Values in {brackets} are maximum possible
Insurgency:  slight unrest -- insurgency growing
Govt Philosophy:   moderate left
Military Power:   Moderate
Sphere of Influence:   Slightly USSR
Govt Stability:    shaky -- weakening fast
Capital: Jakarta              Insurgency: insurgency
```

The government is friendly to me; it will be difficult to improve on this situation. Nevertheless, it is a left-wing government, so if I could topple it, the Soviet score might fall further. There isn't much chance of the insurgency's going anywhere, but there are two weak spots. First, the government is shaky and weakening fast—a coup is in the offing. If I can help that along, I stand to gain. Of course, I could also send in economic aid, save the government, and be the hero. The other possibility lies in their high probability of Finlandizing to me. Perhaps a little diplomatic pressure will yield an act of Finlandization.

The problem with all this is that "Slightly USSR" entry for Sphere of Influence. Anything I try might well be upset by a Soviet challenge. What I need is some way of legitimizing my presence in Indonesia. I need better treaty relations. I therefore decide on a two-pronged strategy. First, I sign a trade-relations pact with Indonesia. Second, I apply a small amount of diplomatic pressure:

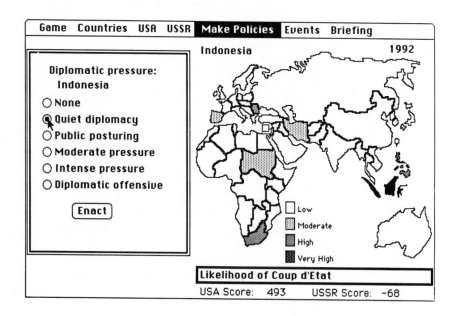

The second policy is risky, but I don't have much time left in the game to take a slower strategy.

I also send some more economic aid to Peru.

TURN 7: SOVIET RESPONSES, AND CONCLUSIONS

The Soviet Union again fails to challenge any of my moves. The game is almost over; the main problem now is to get in a few last changes without doing anything foolish.

*T*URN 8: *1993*

The situation continues to worsen. My score rises, fortunately, but the Soviet score rises even faster; it's now 537 to 178. This is the last turn of the game, and it seems unlikely that they can catch up to me in one turn, but my once-huge lead has shrunk considerably. Even worse is the world situation:

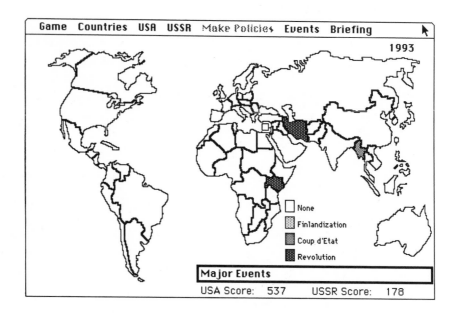

The brutal Soviet invasion of Iran has been victorious; Iran is now a Soviet satellite. The victory actually gains me a little prestige, as the Ayatollah's regime hated America utterly, but the Soviet gain is even greater: 267 points. But that is the only event worthy of note in the year. Otherwise, the world is very quiet. Africa seems to have settled down. There is nothing in the Soviet activities folder that I can challenge, and the only policy action that I undertake is an attempt to destabilize the Indonesian government. The Soviets do not challenge this action when their chance comes, and the game ends.

END OF GAME

Well, I still managed to win the game, and rather well at that:

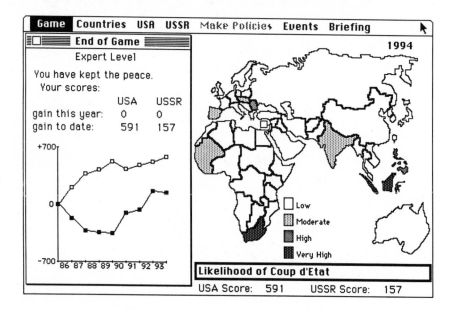

A score of 591 to 157 is pretty respectable. It's not as good as it was halfway through the game, but it's still a score to be pleased with. The final Major Events display looked like this:

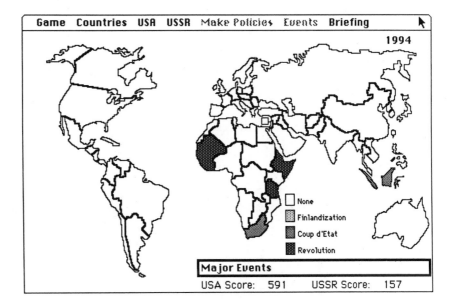

The three most important events in this were the revolution in Ethiopia and the coups in Indonesia and South Africa. All except the last event worked to my favor, which is why my situation improved on the last turn.

ANALYSIS OF HISTORIES

Before I launch into an analysis of the game, it would be worthwhile to look over the individual histories of several countries. This will shed light on a number of crucial developments that I did not see coming during the course of the game.

I will start with Ethiopia:

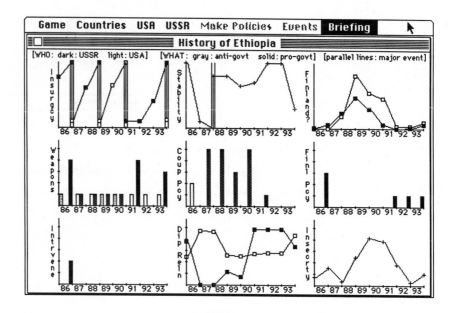

This is definitely one of the most twisted and interesting history charts I have ever seen come out of *Balance of Power.* Ethiopia started the game with a pro-Soviet, left-wing government. (The little black square on the left edge of the "Insurgcy" graph indicates a left-wing government at the beginning of the game.) Then came a series of revolutions and one coup. The revolutions are indicated by the pairs of vertical lines in the "Insurgcy" graph, and the coup is indicated by the pairs of vertical lines in the "Stabilty" graph. The government flipped and flopped back and forth between the left and the right, as indicated by the alternating black and white squares in the "Insurgcy" graph. The Soviets added to the confusion by meddling in matters just enough to keep the pot bubbling but never enough to help its side win once and for all. The first revolution of 1986-87 put a very pro-American government in power, but this was weakened by the coup of 1987-88 and reversed by the revolution of 1990-91. It was the last revolution, in 1993-94, which again reversed the relationship, putting a more pro-American government in power. Thus, despite all the Soviet meddling, the Ethiopian government at the end of the game was more pro-American than the one at the beginning of the game, as indicated by the "Dip Reln" graph.

India provides another example of the ineffectiveness of Soviet meddling, as you can see on the next page.

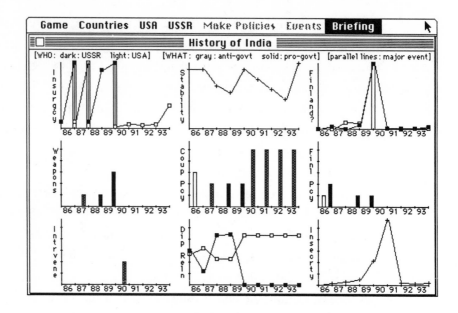

The Indian government entered the game slightly pro-Soviet, but a quick revolution installed a pro-American government. The Soviets shipped some weapons to the insurgents and attempted to destabilize the government, and immediately toppled the government and put the left-wingers back in power. Despite escalating weapons shipments, this left-wing government was thrown out in 1989-90 and replaced with a strong pro-American government. The Soviet weapons shipments to the insurgents in 1989 insured that the new government would be anti-Soviet, and despite an intervention in 1990, the new government proved to be stable. I think that the Soviets would have liked to send more troops into India, but they were badly over-extended and just didn't have the troops to do so.

The reason that my exploratory bid to make a treaty with India in 1991 cost me so many prestige points is now apparent in the "Insecrty" graph in the lower right. Indian insecurity peaked in 1991, probably because of the Soviet intervention in 1990. "Insecurity" on this graph is really a representation of *Military Pressure* from the program's inner workings. You will recall that *Military Pressure* is the degree to which a government feels the need to increase its military budget. As it happens, *Military Pressure* is also used to compute the amount of *Hurt* that any treaty will inflict on a country—although such *Hurt* is always negative. Thus, I walked in and offered safety and security at the precise moment that India was feeling very threatened by the Soviet Union. What I thought was a minor exploratory action turned out to have immense significance to India. At the moment that they felt most in need, the United States stepped forward to offer them the security implicit in a treaty. You can imagine the reaction this generated within the Kremlin, which thought it had a solid grip on India. That is why the Indian crisis proved to be so expensive.

The last history graph I will present is that of Iran, shown on the following page.

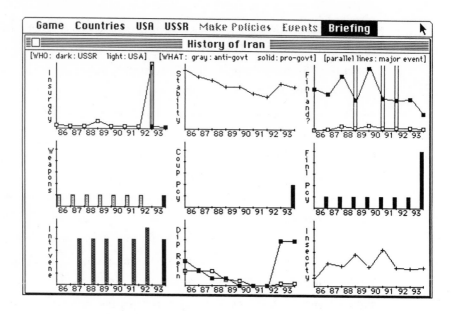

The Soviet invasion in 1987 did not make much of an impression; apparently the Iranian armed forces were able to contain it. The insurgency stayed weak for years. The only real change was in Finlandization. Although the Iranians were winning on the battlefield, the growing strain between the superpowers and the demonstrated willingness of the Soviets to engage in harsh actions must have convinced the Iranian leadership that Finlandization was necessary to buy off the Soviets. Three times they Finlandized to the USSR. Each time, diplomatic relations with the US worsened, and each time relations with the Soviet Union improved, only to be immediately ruined when the Soviets nevertheless refused to pull out their troops. The big break came in 1992 when the Kremlin finally scraped up half a million men to finish off Iran. That produced the revolution of 1992-93 and a dramatic improvement in relations between the two countries, with positive consequences for Soviet prestige.

FINAL ANALYSIS

So what does it all mean? In the first half of the game, I pursued a conservative strategy of protecting only those nations about which I felt secure. Most of the critical actions were taken on Turn 1. After that, I just protected my gains. However, my lead lengthened considerably on Turns 2 through 4. Why?

I believe that the Soviet Union involved itself in too many adventures and did not have the resources to make its plans work. The primary cause for this lay in their repeated unexpected failures in crises. My conservative strategy insured that I won many crises and lost very few. This not only enhanced my prestige, it increased my pugnacity in the eyes of the world. This in turn created a considerable tendency to Finlandize to the United States during Turns 2 through 4. The Soviets had already committed themselves to extensive operations in Africa, and suddenly their own allies were starting to waver. At various points in the game almost every single Eastern bloc country showed an inclination to Finlandize to the USA. To counter this, the Kremlin had to rush troops and weapons to the threatened countries to bolster their confidence. Unfortunately, these troops and weapons were desperately needed to follow through on the various adventures in Africa, India, and Iran. For example, the Soviets shipped enough weapons to the government of Ethiopia to earn the enmity of the insurgents who beat that government, but they were not able to ship enough weapons to throw out those right-wingers or, later, protect the left-wing government that eventually came back to power.

The Soviet shortages continued as long as I kept up the pressure, but by midgame things were calming down and I was having few confrontations with the USSR. I thought that I was preserving my lead, but in fact I was taking the pressure off the Soviet allies, and hence the Soviets. They were able to commit more resources to cement their gains. Thus we have the large Soviet weapons shipments to Ethiopia in 1991 and the huge invasion of Iran in 1992. The impact of this Soviet freedom to act shows in the score display: After bottoming out in 1989-90, the Soviet score starts to rise sharply.

I made several mistakes. Obviously, I should have kept up the pressure through the middle of the game, although there is no way of knowing whether this might not have driven the Soviets to desperate measures. I should definitely have developed my Indonesian initiative sooner. It also might have been possible to take some action in Iran sooner. A friendly gesture to the Iranians might well have brought them into my arms as their savior. Finally, I should not have surrendered Africa so easily at the beginning of the game. Granted, the Soviets began with a large advantage; I could have developed my position in Kenya and possibly Tanzania. I was just not thinking in terms of a long-term strategy for that region.

BIBLIOGRAPHY

I thought that I had put a lot of research into the original game, but this book required even more. Thus, while this bibliography features many works for the game, it contains more works not included there.

PROBLEMS OF THE MODERN WORLD

Boyd, Andrew. *An Atlas of World Affairs.* 7th ed. London and New York: Methuen, 1983. Covers each region of the world, discussing its political issues and how it affects the global equation. Not as insightful as Dunnigan's book, but a good second opinion.

Chant, Christopher, and Hogg, Ian. *Nuclear War in the 1980's?* New York: Harper and Row, 1983. Lots of colorful pictures of rockets, guns, airplanes, and so forth. Some elementary information on the mechanics of nuclear war. Average text entry is only one page long. Get this for your teenager.

Council on Environmental Quality. *The Global 2000 Report to the President.* New York: Penguin Books, 1982. Lots and lots of hard data on declining resources of all kinds.

Dunnigan, James F. *How to Make War.* New York: Morrow, 1982. An excellent description of the mechanics of modern warfare.

Dunnigan, James F., and Bay, Austin. *A Quick and Dirty Guide to War.* New York: Morrow, 1985. Subtitled *Briefings on Present and Potential Wars,* this book is loaded with solid information on the wars going on around the world.

Gervasi, Tom. *America's War Machine*. New York: Grove Press, 1984. The *Whole Earth Catalog* of weapons systems. A strong anti-militaristic tone pervades the book.

Griffiths, Ieuan. *An Atlas of African Affairs*. London and New York: Methuen, 1984. A treatment focusing on Africa and its problems.

Ground Zero. *What About the Russians—and Nuclear War?* New York: Pocket Books, 1983. A balanced and careful discussion of the Soviet Union—its people, government, history, and psychology—and how these factors affect Soviet nuclear policy. Recommended reading.

Kaplan, Fred. *The Wizards of Armageddon*. New York: Simon and Schuster, 1983. The story of the think-tank people who developed the strategies for nuclear war. An interesting exposition of how our thinking on nuclear war has developed. These people figured out *how* to fight nuclear war without ever asking *why* we should fight— that wasn't their job, I suppose.

Kennan, George F. *The Nuclear Delusion*. New York: Pantheon, 1982.

Kidron, Michael, and Segal, Ronald. *The State of the World Atlas*. New York: Simon and Schuster, 1981. Similar to *The War Atlas*, but more general in the themes it addresses: natural resources, economy, government, society, and so forth.

Kidron, Michael, and Smith, Dan. *The War Atlas*. New York: Simon and Schuster, 1983. Forty multicolored maps showing the factors affecting war and peace in the world of the 1980s. The strong graphics make esoteric factors more understandable. This book was the inspiration for the map-intensive display of *Balance of Power.* I only wish I had as many colors as they do.

Kissinger, Henry. *The White House Years* and *Years of Upheaval.* Boston: Little, Brown and Company, 1979 and 1982. Whether or not you agreed with Dr. Kissinger's policies, you will find these two books immensely informative on the workings of superpower diplomacy. Fascinating reading, highly recommended.

Millar, T. B. *The East-West Strategic Balance.* Winchester, MA: Allen & Unwin, 1981. A region-by-region analysis of the geopolitical positions and strengths of the two superpowers.

Pluto-Maspero Project. *World View 1982.* Boston: South End Press, 1982. "An economic and geopolitical yearbook" with a decidedly left-wing slant. Americans who do not understand European leftist anxieties about American policies should read this with an open but not gullible mind.

Spector, Leonard S. *Nuclear Proliferation Today.* New York: Vintage Books, 1984. I didn't include proliferation in the game, and I'm glad I didn't—you'd never win! This book should scare you. Lots of detailed information on how and why the nuclear genie is out of the bottle.

Suvorov, Viktor. *Inside the Soviet Army.* New York: Macmillan, 1982. A defector talks about how the Soviet Army functions. Scary business; these people are not sweetie pies!

ACADEMIC ANALYSES

Allison, Graham T. *Essence of Decision: Explaining the Cuban Missile Crisis.* Boston: Little, Brown and Company, 1971. An analysis of the logical, political, and bureaucratic factors that led to the Cuban missile crisis and its resolution.

Bueno de Mesquita, Bruce. *The War Trap.* New Haven: Yale University Press, 1981. A theoretical work that attempts to establish a mathematically rigorous theory explaining how seemingly reasonable national policies tend to trap nations into wars. Lots of equations for you math types. In the end, I elected not to use the very impressive mathematical results; I just couldn't work them in.

Howard, Michael. *The Causes of Wars.* Cambridge, MA: Harvard University Press, 1984. A series of essays by a noted historian. Thought-provoking, but somewhat advanced for the general reader.

Levy, Jack S. *War in the Modern Great Power System.* Lexington: University Press of Kentucky, 1983. A statistical analysis of 119 major wars fought in the last 500 years. Some things have changed and some things have not.

Luttwak, Edward. *Coup d'Etat: A Practical Handbook.* 2d ed. Cambridge, MA: Harvard University Press, 1979. An academic analysis presented in the form of a detailed handbook on the strategy and tactics of the modern coup. Purportedly used by at least one unsuccessful plotter.

Pimlott, John, ed. *Guerrilla Warfare.* New York: The Military Press, 1985. A big picture book with some surprisingly astute analysis of the theory of guerrilla war.

Prados, John. *The Soviet Estimate.* New York: Dial Press, 1982. A history of American assessment of Russian military strength. We always seemed to overestimate them.

Taylor, Charles Lewis, and Jodice, David A. *World Handbook of Political and Social Indicators.* New Haven: Yale University Press, 1983. A two-volume compilation of numbers about the nations of the world. This is a scholarly work, not for general readers. Nevertheless, the numbers are fascinating.

HISTORY

Burns, Thomas. *A History of the Ostrogoths.* Bloomington: Indiana University Press, 1984. I went through this book trying to get a good quote about feudal Finlandization and failed.

Caesar, Julius. *The Conquest of Gaul.* Translated by S. A. Hanford. New York: Penguin, 1951. He came, he conquered, he wrote.

Fair, Charles. *From the Jaws of Victory.* New York: Simon and Schuster, 1971. One of the truly great books about war. The chapter on Charles XII of Sweden, and especially its conclusion, affected me greatly.

Ferrill, Arther. *The Origins of War: From the Stone Age to Alexander the Great.* New York: Thames and Hudson (dist. by W. W. Norton), 1985. The origins of war, up to the time of Alexander. Concentrates on military strategy and tactics, not the reasons why we started this insanity.

Gregory of Tours. *The History of the Franks.* Translated by Lewis Thorpe. New York: Penguin, 1974. Franks kill Franks as saintly author tut-tuts. They *did* have some great names: Childebert, Theudebert, Theudebald, Chilperic, Sigibert, and Chlodomer. Seeking names for that new child?

Kennedy, Robert F. *Thirteen Days.* New York: Norton, 1969. A very personal memoir of the Cuban missile crisis.

Luckenbill, D. D. *Ancient Records of Assyria and Babylonia.* 2 volumes. Chicago: University of Chicago Press, 1927; reprint: Westport, CT: Greenwood Press, 1969.

Machiavelli, Niccolo. *The Prince.* Translated by George Bull. New York: Penguin, 1961. Described as "the Bible of *realpolitik,*" this little book contains much common sense about the art of ruling, but is too closely tied to Renaissance Italy to be of great relevance today.

Maenchen-Helfen, Otto J. *The World of the Huns: Studies in Their History and Culture.* Berkeley: University of California Press, 1973. Who would have thought that Attila the Hun could be boring? Very academic.

Shirer, William L. *The Rise and Fall of the Third Reich.* New York: Fawcett, 1950. The whole bloody story, frightening in its details.

Thucydides. *History of the Peloponnesian War.* Translated by Rex Warner. New York: Penguin Books, 1954. Greeks fight Greeks in this long history.

Tuchman, Barbara W. *The Guns of August.* New York: Macmillan, 1962. A history of the events leading up to the outbreak of World War I and the first months of fighting. Good reading.

Ulam, Adam B. *Russia's Failed Revolutions: From the Decembrists to the Dissidents.* New York: Basic Books, 1981.

CHRIS CRAWFORD

Chris Crawford is one of today's leading computer game designers. In addition to "Balance of Power," he is the creator of such games as "Energy Czar," "Scram," "Eastern Front," and "Excalibur." Chris is also the author of *The Art of Computer Game Design*, published in 1984. He presently lives in San Jose, California.

The manuscript for this book was prepared and
submitted to Microsoft Press in electronic form.
Text files were processed and formatted using
Microsoft Word.

Cover and interior text design by Rikki Conrad Design

Cover and interior illustrations by David Shannon

Principal typographer: Christopher Banks

Principal production artist: Becky Johnson

The high-resolution screen displays were created on
the Apple Macintosh Plus and printed on
the Apple LaserWriter.

Text composition by Microsoft Press in Bauer Bodoni
and display in Bauer Bodoni Italic, using the CCI-400
composition system and the Mergenthaler Linotron
202 digital phototypesetter.